Sulky, Rowdy, Rude?

by the same author

No Fighting, No Biting, No Screaming
How to Make Behaving Positively Possible for People with
Autism and Other Developmental Disabilities
Bo Hejlskov Elvén
ISBN 978 1 84905 126 2
eISBN 978 0 85700 322 5

Frightened, Disturbed, Dangerous?
Why working with patients in psychiatric care can
be really difficult, and what to do about it
Bo Hejlskov Elvén and Sophie Abild McFarlane
ISBN 978 1 78592 214 5
eISBN 978 1 78450 493 9

Disruptive, Stubborn, Out of Control?
Why kids get confrontational in the classroom,
and what to do about it
Bo Hejlskov Elvén
ISBN 978 1 78592 212 1
eISBN 978 1 78450 490 8

Confused, Angry, Anxious?
Why working with older people in care really can
be difficult, and what to do about it
Bo Hejlskov Elvén, Charlotte Agger, and Iben Ljungmann
ISBN 978 1 78592 215 2
eISBN 978 1 78450 494 6

SULKY ROWDY RUDE?

Why kids really act out
+ what to do about it

Bo Hejlskov Elvén and Tina Wiman

Jessica Kingsley *Publishers*
London and Philadelphia

First published in 2017
by Jessica Kingsley Publishers
73 Collier Street
London N1 9BE, UK
and
400 Market Street, Suite 400
Philadelphia, PA 19106, USA

www.jkp.com

Library of Congress Cataloging in Publication Data
Names: Elven, Bo Hejlskov, author. | Wiman, Tina, author.
Title: Sulky, rowdy, rude : why kids really act out and what to do about it /
    Bo Hejlskov Elven and Tina Wiman.
Description: London ; Philadelphia : Jessica Kingsley Publishers, 2017.
Identifiers: LCCN 2016033363 (print) | LCCN 2016047579 (ebook) | ISBN
    9781785922138 (alk. paper) | ISBN 9781784504922 (ebook)
Subjects: LCSH: Problem children. | Problem children--Behavior modification.
    | Parenting.
Classification: LCC HQ773 .E456 2017 (print) | LCC HQ773 (ebook) | DDC
    649/.153--dc23

British Library Cataloguing in Publication Data
A CIP catalogue record for this book is available from the British Library.

ISBN: 978 1 78592 213 8
eISBN: 978 1 78450 492 2

Printed and bound in Great Britain

Contents

Introduction   7

Part 1: Principles

1   Who Has the Problem?   13

2   Children Behave Well If They Can   18

3   Children Always Do What Makes Sense   30

4   The One Who Takes Responsibility Can Make a Difference   35

5   Children Learn Nothing from Failure   50

6   You Need Self-control to Cooperate with Others   57

7   We All Do What We Can to Maintain Self-control   67

8   Emotions Are Contagious   72

9   Conflicts Consist of Solutions and Failures Require a Plan   85

10   We Make Demands of Children That They Don't
     Make of Themselves – But in a Way That Works   91

11   It Isn't Fair to Treat Everyone the Same   101

12   You Become a Leader When Someone Follows You   105

Part 2: Cases and Action Plans

13   We Live in a Garage   113

14   Case Examples   117

15   The Principle of the Gentle Approach   156

16   Summary   164

Part 3: Extra Materials

Study Materials   169

Further Reading   178

Introduction

Becoming a parent is an exciting journey into a new experience. New and not always easy. You and your children will often want different things. And what does one do when the baby won't eat, when the schoolchild refuses to do his homework or the teenager doesn't come home till the early hours of the morning? From the time that our children are small till the time they grow up, conflicts are as ever present as reasons for joy.

Conflicts and arguments are nothing exceptional, but rather a part of everyday family life. As parents, we do the best we can to sort things out and most of the time it turns out OK. With the great majority of children, using perfectly normal methods works well enough, even those that actually don't seem to work according to scientific research. You ride out the storm and that's all there is to it. But sometimes we get stuck in patterns of behaviour which fill our everyday life with a disproportionate amount of strife. Then we need to take a look at how we are treating our children – what methods we are actually using. Perhaps they are ineffective – or even make the situation worse.

Conflict can, of course, present in different ways. The small child might cry, scratch or kick, while the teenager shouts, slams doors and swears. One child fights, another runs away. A third child throws chairs around. And then there are children who end up in conflict more often than others, with their parents, siblings and friends. These children need especially good parents and especially good methods. But, unfortunately, it's often the other way around. These are the children who are most often scolded, sent to their rooms or punished in other ways – even though this rarely helps.

It is easy to think that parents need to take control over their children – especially if they fight a lot. But this is actually not meaningful at all. Instead, as adults we need to be in control of *ourselves*. Children will acquire greater self-control as they grow older, but it's difficult when they are small; that's why they may need a little more help from us in order to manage everyday life.

That's what this book is about: how as parents we can help our little children, bigger children and teenagers take control and *stay* in control of themselves; how we can create structures, methods and situations that work, so that children can do what they need to do, at the same time as they feel security, belonging and autonomy, and practise self-control and cooperation – so that they, in turn, can become adults who have control over themselves.

In the long run, no parents want obedient children. The present authors, at least, have never met any parents who hoped that their children would grow up into obedient adults. Obedience isn't a very good quality to take with you into adult life. On the contrary, parents want their children to learn to make wise decisions, to take responsibility for their own lives and to cooperate with others. So these are the skills we need to practise with our children.

This is a book about difficult situations, and not least, about children who are difficult for us to manage as parents.

This book is not going to be about rewards, punishments and consequences; nor do we talk about will or motivation, about children challenging us parents, or about them being able to challenge us if they only want. All of these are misunderstandings that are built on incorrect assumptions about children's abilities. Instead, we start from the assumption that all children want to succeed, even children who act out. Our focus is on helping parents make everyday life simple enough and manageable enough for their children to have the opportunity to grow and develop.

The methods and approaches that are discussed have been developed in work with children and adults with diagnoses. The methods are based on what we in Sweden refer to as the *low-arousal approach*. This is an approach which at its origin has to do with managing people who are violent in such a way that no one gets hurt and the level of violence diminishes. Occasionally in the text we will refer to scientific research in the context of the low-arousal approach. If you want to read more, you will find references and suggestions for further reading collected at the end of the book.

We have lengthy experience in working with children with diagnoses, Bo Hejlskov Elvén as a psychologist and Tina Wiman as a specialist in the field of information technology support for children with special needs. But we also have experience as parents. We have children both with and without diagnoses, and we have seen that the methods we describe in the book work just as well with or without a diagnosis. Many children with a tendency to act out sometimes react by arguing, fighting or throwing furniture around. In that situation the important thing is not whether the child has a diagnosis or not. That's why we don't discuss it in the book. The important thing is that as parents we know what to do when such situations arise – and that we know how to prevent similar situations from arising in the future.

THE STRUCTURE OF THE BOOK

Part 1 is divided into 12 chapters, each dealing with one principle, one basic concept. Some of them are quite far from how we as parents normally think about children. For each principle, we give at least one example of an everyday conflict. The idea is to explain how and why disagreement develops into fighting, and what we as parents can change in order to turn the development around. We hope that you will gain some new ideas and be curious and open enough to try them out for yourself, because it is only in your own everyday life that you can see what a difference your approach can make.

In the second part of the book there are more examples from everyday life. Using the principles in the first part, we now take a closer look at what is really happening in the different situations, and what strategies and methods one can make use of as a parent.

In Part 3, at the end of the book there is a reference section for those who want to know more about the research behind the low-arousal approach. There are also study materials which can be used as a basis for discussion, for example with your partner or in a group of parents.

Parenthood is an exciting and challenging journey. On the way, as parents we sometimes need to confront ourselves and our way of thinking. We need to reflect on what we do that works and what we want to change.

Hopefully this book can help you discover new paths on your parenting journey and make daily life simpler, calmer and better – both for your children and yourself.

Part 1

Principles

1

Who Has the Problem?

KATIE

Katie knows that she is a girl. It's very important to her. She also knows that girls usually wear dresses. So she has a clear principle: she wants to wear a dress.

This morning Katie is woken up by her father, Mark. When it's time to get her clothes on, she finds a dress in the wardrobe and puts it on. Her father Mark has no problem with this, as long as she also wears tights. After all, it's well below zero outside. Katie agrees and happily puts on her favourite tights, the striped ones.

When it's time to go to day care Mark holds out her snowsuit. But then Katie's face falls. She doesn't want to wear that. When you're wearing a dress, you obviously can't wear a snowsuit. Katie's father won't give in; he wants her to wear the snowsuit. So Katie yells, 'No!' and runs and hides. When Mark finds her, she swipes at him and says: 'I hate you!'

Mark gets angry. Katie shouldn't hit him. She should do what she is told. So he takes hold of Katie, drags her to the entrance hall and puts the snowsuit on her. She fights back and manages to free one arm. In the end Mark has to hold her arm quite tightly in order to get the suit on. Then they go out to the car and drive off to day care. Katie cries the whole way there. She's sulky and doesn't want to say goodbye when her father leaves to go to work.

KATIE AND MARK'S PROBLEM

Who is really the one with a problem in the situation described above? This is an important question to ask if the goal is not only to stop the current fight but also to prevent a similar situation from arising again the next morning.

In the example above, neither Katie nor Mark has a problem in the beginning. The first person to encounter a problem is Mark. This happens when Katie suddenly refuses to put on her snowsuit. At this time Katie still doesn't have a problem. That only happens when Mark sticks to his demand about the snowsuit. She solves her problem by hiding. But Mark's problem is still unsolved.

Katie's options in this situation are limited, but she feels that she has the right to react to what she sees as an injustice. The means she has available are crying, hiding, saying she hates her father and swiping at him. She manages a difficult situation in any way she can. She tries to solve her problem using the means available to her.

If Mark works on the assumption that Katie is the one who is making a fuss and creating a problem, then things are going to get difficult. Because that means he wants Katie to change. But Katie doesn't think that her behaviour is a problem. She is unable to see how she could change her solution. Mark is an adult. Katie is 4 years old. Therefore, both Mark's motivation and his ability to change the situation must be greater than Katie's motivation.

Mark must also figure out how he can ensure that the same thing doesn't happen again. To put the snowsuit on

Katie by force is not a good solution. It means that he uses up some of his parental capital and that Katie's confidence in him needs to be rebuilt. In the situation above, Katie learns nothing except that her opinion is of no value and that her father can do whatever he wants with her. This is probably not what Mark actually wanted her to learn.

WHY IT IS NOT THE CHILD'S RESPONSIBILITY TO SOLVE OUR PROBLEMS

In this book we describe methods that parents can use in order to handle problems and conflicts that arise in everyday life with children. But it is vitally important right from the start to point out that the focus is on differentiating between which problems are ours and which are the child's.

As a rule, children try to solve their problems using all the means available to them. Sometimes it works, and sometimes it doesn't work very well. They are, after all, children and not as good at managing their everyday life, their feelings and their lives as we adults are. We know that we have a greater responsibility than children do, and that they need our help.

This may seem obvious, but in practice we often act on the assumption that children should be able to sharpen up and change the situation – especially when problems arise.

But children usually behave like children. It is therefore important that we adults behave like adults. Only by taking responsibility can we solve the problems we come across in everyday life with our children.

OLIVER
Oliver is sitting at the computer. It's getting close to bedtime and his mother, Lisa, asks him to turn it off. 'I'm just going to finish this level,' he says. But Lisa doesn't agree. 'Turn it

off now. It's ten o'clock and time for you to brush your teeth and go to bed.'

Lisa goes back to the living room. Oliver carries on playing in his room. After a while, he has finished the level he was on, but then he starts on a new one. After 10 minutes Lisa comes back: 'I told you to turn it off! If you don't do what I tell you, I'll turn off the Internet.' Lisa doesn't know that Oliver is not online. So he keeps playing. After a while, Lisa pulls out the Internet plug. But Oliver keeps on playing. Then Lisa explodes: 'Now that's enough! You are completely hopeless! Go and brush your teeth *now*! Otherwise, I'll drag you to the bathroom!'

Oliver goes and brushes his teeth. Then he says goodnight, takes the computer with him under the blanket and carries on playing.

STRATEGIES

In Oliver's case, there are also good reasons for his behaviour. It's difficult for him to turn off the computer in the middle of a level, just as most adults would have difficulty leaving a cinema after half a movie just because someone told us to leave. He also can't resist the temptation to carry on playing once the level is completed. Oliver's argument is not taken seriously by his mother, and he keeps on playing.

Lisa's problem is that Oliver won't turn off the computer. Oliver's problem is that Lisa is asking him to turn it off. This means that they have two different problems and see two different solutions. To expect Oliver to understand and solve Lisa's problem is probably not realistic. Lisa must therefore find a way to solve her problem, a way that is not dependent on what Oliver wants or does.

In the situation above, Lisa thinks that Oliver should solve her problem. But if he doesn't do as Lisa wants, then she becomes powerless – and that is the worst possible feeling to have. No parent wants to feel that way. That's why, in the rest of the book, we are going to investigate how we as parents can avoid ending up in such situations.

Summary

Adults often describe children's behaviour by saying they cause trouble. They feel that a problem exists, but children don't feel that way – and children who don't see or think that there is a problem are seldom motivated to change their behaviour. That's why it is the adult's responsibility to change the situation so that conflicts don't arise.

2

Children Behave Well If They Can

THOMAS

Thomas is 8 years old. He is at Legoland® with his parents and his sister. Thomas has been looking forward to the visit to Legoland for a long time. He has nagged insistently about coming here, and now it has finally happened. His father, Eric, leads the family towards the Minilands that they have talked about at home and that Thomas has wanted to see. But now that they are finally here, all that Thomas sees are the rides. After a while he starts complaining: 'Can't we go on the rollercoaster now? This is boring.'

Eric tells him that first they're going to look at the cities and landscapes in peace and quiet. That's why they came here, after all. 'Going on rollercoasters is something we can do anywhere', he says. 'You won't find the Legoland Minilands anywhere else. You've been nagging for ages to come here and look at them, haven't you?'

Thomas gets more and more impatient and says to Eric: 'But we might not have time to go on the rollercoaster if we don't go now.' Eric says he's sure they will have time to do everything. They have a long day ahead of them. At last Thomas says: 'Then I'll go there on my own'. 'No you won't, you're staying here!' says Eric, taking hold of Thomas' arm. But Thomas pulls free and runs away. In a moment he has disappeared.

Eric runs to the rollercoaster, but he can't find Thomas. After quarter of an hour, he goes to the Information and asks them to call for Thomas on the public-address system. But this doesn't help, since Thomas doesn't hear it. After a couple of hours, Thomas' family finally catch sight of him. He's upset and stressed over not having been able to find his parents.

ABILITIES, DEMANDS AND EXPECTATIONS

The principle 'Children behave well if they can' was formulated by American psychologist Ross W. Greene. It's actually quite simple. If a child behaves well, it's because he can. If a child doesn't behave well, it's because he can't – in which case those around him must start to think about whether their expectations of the child's abilities are too high.

In Thomas' case, the parents are asking a lot of him during the visit to Legoland®, even if they are not aware of it. To start with, they expect Thomas to be able to differentiate between needs and impulses. He wants to see the Minilands; this we can call a need. Before the trip, they had talked a lot about how nicely the landscapes had been constructed. But when Thomas arrives at the amusement park, the impulse to immediately go on the rollercoaster becomes so strong that he can't resist it. His parents still expect him to be able to control his behaviour in line with the plan they have made together for Legoland. They also expect him to be able to obey, in a situation where he is in a new place with a lot of people.

But the stress that being at Legoland causes for Thomas makes it difficult for him to manage. So he does his best, but it doesn't turn out so well. He begins to nag. In the resulting situation, Thomas' father doesn't want his authority challenged. He escalates the conflict by taking hold of Thomas. But this only increases Thomas' feeling of powerlessness, so he pulls free and runs away.

All in all, we can conclude that Thomas has trouble with readjusting his expectations, with being part of a bigger context, with structuring and calculating the day's activities and with foreseeing the consequences of his actions, especially in a new and different environment. He does his best throughout the situation. It just isn't good enough.

Thomas is by no means an unusual child. Most children have some difficulty in getting everyday life to hang together, and not least with things that lie outside of the normal routine. Exactly what it is that is difficult varies from child to child. In the example with Thomas, it is clear that the demands that are being placed on his abilities are simply too high.

What is a demand?
In this book we talk a lot about demands. By 'demands' we mean not only what parents tell children to do, such as making the bed or coming to eat; we also mean other, unspoken demands and expectations which, for example, depend on how we as parents behave in a certain situation, what other people say and do, or on the physical environment.

A good example of an unspoken demand is when we use long sentences to explain things. Using many words places high demands on the child's language abilities and memory, regardless of whether we are talking about something boring, like cleaning, or offering something nice, like ice cream. Most of us are aware of this when it comes to very small children, and so we use much shorter sentences and simpler language with babies than we do with 10-year-olds, because 10-year-olds simply have a much greater ability to understand what we are saying – at least as long as they are calm.

The environment we are in also places demands on children's abilities. An amusement park such as Legoland®, with lots of noise, movement and people, places demands on their ability to sort and interpret many different impressions simultaneously – and an upset sibling who is shouting or crying places demands on their ability to remain calm and ignore disturbing noises.

So the demands that are placed on children's abilities consist partly of the things that we as parents aim for our children to do, and partly of all the other things that they need to absorb, interpret and handle in a particular situation.

Further along in this chapter, we will consider various abilities with which children sometimes struggle. When we as parents overestimate such abilities, it often ends in conflict. A couple of these abilities are so important that we will devote entire chapters to them. But first let's talk a little about who the children are that act out.

CHARACTERISTICS AND NORMAL DISTRIBUTION

Human characteristics are often distributed in what we call a 'normal distribution'. This applies to characteristics such as height, weight, intelligence, attentiveness, the ability to structure, the ability to learn, the ability to wait, social skills and a host of others. The normal distribution of human characteristics is often illustrated as shown in Figure 2.1.

Normal distribution means that most people lie around the average, and the further you move from the average, the fewer you find.

Figure 2.1 should be seen as a group of people placed on a line based on a given characteristic, for example height. The short people are shown on the *left* and the tall ones on the *right*. There are not many of the very shortest or the very tallest people. In the middle are those of average height. There are so many of them that they would have to stand on each other's shoulders in order to fit. In other words, the illustration shows that most people's characteristics lie around the average. The further you go from the average, regardless of direction, the fewer people you will find. This is easy to understand when it comes to height, but exactly the same thing applies for all the abilities that the situation in Legoland® demanded of Thomas.

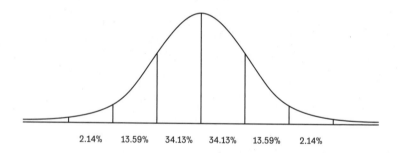

2.14%   13.59%   34.13%   34.13%   13.59%   2.14%

Figure 2.1 The normal distribution of human characteristics

All children are good at different things. So, in a group of perfectly normal families, there will be a couple of children who can handle a deviation from daily routine very well, many who handle it well, some who handle it fairly well and a few who have major problems when everyday life makes new demands of them. Their mood on the day and other personal factors will also play a role. Most children can handle unexpected situations better when they feel secure and do not feel stressed.

If a child is far enough below the average in a number of abilities, then the risk (or chance) increases that the child will be given a diagnosis. However, there is a gradual transition between diagnosis and normality. Children have both strengths and weaknesses; they find some things easy and others much harder. And actually that's one of the things we parents love most about our children: that they are different and have little idiosyncrasies that are entirely their own.

HOW CHILDREN HAVE DIFFERENT LEVELS OF POTENTIAL

A central theme in this book is that children have different levels of potential. When we talk about trouble and conflicts with children, we are actually talking about which children have the potential to live up to the demands that the adult world places on them, and which children do not. The reasons why some children don't manage to live up to demands and expectations can be many. It may be, for example, that they lack the abilities, that they are stressed, have difficult relationships or have insufficient security in their everyday life. So, in this book we don't talk about children's will to behave or their motives. The most important reason for this is that research has shown that if we act on the basis of Greene's principle – 'Children behave well if they can' – then we get a better result.

WHY CONFLICT IS A PART OF EVERYDAY LIFE

Sometimes parents speak about children acting out as if it were something out of the ordinary – but it is not. Conflict is a part of everyday life. There will always be situations with children that don't go the way we plan or want. But every time a situation goes badly, we should sit down and think through the situation step by step. What actually happened? When did we place demands on the child that were too high? What was it that he couldn't cope with?

If we don't go through the events properly, then there is a risk that we will focus only on what the child should have done, instead of what he actually did. And then we are guaranteed to have a problem again the next time we end up in a similar situation.

To see our own role in our children's behaviour may feel difficult. But it is still absolutely essential for us to gain insight into how we affect our children, in order for a situation not to be repeated.

So what we have to do is think about our own behaviour as parents and our own expectations of the child's abilities, and then compare our expectations with the child's real abilities, what they are really able to do. Then it will be easier to see where the problem lies. In every situation where children have not behaved ideally, we will find something that we adults didn't succeed with in the conflict situation. That's how it is. It may be hard to accept, but it's true.

We are also responsible for the demands that the situation itself places on the child's abilities.

All human behaviour occurs as an interaction with the surrounding environment. There may be other people who affect behaviour, either by what they do and how they do it, or by just being nearby. The physical environment also affects behaviour. The environment can be safe or insecure, noisy or restful, threatening or calm. And, since we adults have greater possibilities to influence both our own behaviour and our environment, it is our responsibility to regulate the child's interaction with the environment.

TOO HIGH EXPECTATIONS

Conflicts arise when a situation places too high demands on a child's abilities. There is much that can go wrong. Perhaps our demands were too high on the ability to create structure, perhaps on impulse control, or on the child's social skills. When we review a conflict situation after it has happened, it is important to think about which of the child's abilities we expected too much of. Only when we understand this can we make sure that the situation does not happen again. Perhaps it was one of many capabilities of the child:

- Ability to calculate cause and effect in complex situations
  We humans need this ability in order to predict the consequences of our own actions, but also in order to form an overall picture of what is about to happen. Children who have difficulty with this need much more structure and predictability than others do. Most people have this ability by the age of 8–10 years, but some never learn it. Instead, they often blame someone else when something goes wrong. Unfortunately, explaining to them doesn't help; it's the matter of a lacking ability, not a failure to understand.

- Ability to structure, plan and carry out activities
  Many children are unable to form an overview of, for example, a morning. They can't plan what they are going to do and they don't know how much time there is left. Some children have trouble with this just because they are too young, but others have difficulty long after others of their own age have learned this skill.

- Ability to remember while thinking

  This is usually called 'working memory'. No small child is able to both remember and process the information they have in their heads at the same time. Towards the teenage years, most children have developed their working memory, but some continue to have difficulties well into adult life. For a child with a poor working memory, we as parents cannot use oral instructions covering several steps; instead, we may need to write down or draw a picture of what the child is to do. Another way is to give one instruction at a time. Perhaps we need to be there the whole way, and keep reminding the child in order for something to get finished.

- Ability to control impulses

  Many children react directly to whatever is happening in a situation and simply can't restrain an impulse when it arises. Children under 6 years of age will, for example, say whatever comes to mind, take hold of something that looks exciting or hit someone. Even as adults we have difficulty in fully controlling our impulses. You as a reader, for example, will think of the colour red if we write that you mustn't think of it. You have difficulty restraining thought impulses. But there are also children who, after the age of 6 years, continue to have difficulty in not acting on impulses. That's why we as parents need to think about what impulses we are creating in them. What rules do we have in our family? How do we treat our children? We must avoid rules and reprimands that have to do with things children must not do, since they create an impulse to do those things. Little children do the things we tell them not to do. For example, if we tell a 3-year-old to stop drumming, then he will have to drum a little more. He can't help it – because the reprimand gave him the impulse.

- Endurance
  Some children have much greater difficulty waiting than others do. The same children often have difficulty in performing activities that require concentration over a long period of time.

- Ability to be flexible or to readjust quickly
  Most children like it when things are the same as usual, and some have huge problems managing change. This is true even when the changes are unavoidable and we think they are just being silly. These children need to know what is going to happen well in advance. We often think they are just being stubborn, but actually they are having a hard time changing their inner perception of what is going to happen.

- Social abilities, such as predicting other people's thoughts, feelings and actions
  Some children have tremendous difficulty seeing their own role in a situation that goes badly, or understanding how the situation and their own behaviour are perceived and interpreted by others. They can also have difficulty understanding other people's intentions. So they end up in conflict with friends and siblings more often than other children do.

- Ability to handle stress
  We differ in how much stress we can take. Some children are easily stressed and lose grasp of situations that others can handle without difficulty.

- Ability to say yes

  It may sound strange, but some children over 3 years of age say yes to most things in life, while others say no. This is a personality trait which is difficult to alter, but it *is* possible to compensate for it. If we have children who have difficulty saying yes, then we need to increase their sense of participation by, for example, giving them more choices. When children under 3 years of age say no most of the time, it's usually because our demands come too suddenly for them. They say no just to be on the safe side. In other words, it's not defiance, even though we call it 'the age of defiance'. If we simply wait for a little while, most often we will eventually get a yes.

- Ability to calm down or to remain calm

  This is called the ability to regulate affect and has to do with how good we are at controlling our emotions. This varies from person to person and increases with age for most people. It is important to remember that this is an ability, not a matter of will. No one wants to lose control over their feelings. Children with strong feelings are often children who have difficulty regulating affect.

Every time our children have a conflict with us or with other children that requires our investigation, we should make a plan to avoid having it happen again. What should normal, everyday life be like in order to reduce the risk of conflict? Sometimes it's a matter of rethinking established routines.

Do children really have to brush all their teeth at the same time? Can we structure the time around meal preparation better, when everyone is tired and hungry? Can the adults in the family divide the work in such a way that one is responsible for keeping the children occupied while the other deals with the practical work? Can we plan and prepare outings and trips a little better, so that children like Thomas know what is going to happen and have a better overview of the day?

ADJUSTMENT OF DEMANDS

There are lots of things that adults can do which children cannot do. Sometimes as parents we have trouble remembering this. Rewards, punishments and consequences are based on the assumption that children can do things if only they have the will to do them. This in turn is a misunderstanding based on false assumptions about children's abilities. That is why they so often go wrong. Such an assumption also makes love conditional: 'If you don't behave, then you won't get my love and appreciation, my rewards or my praise.' Such methods create insecure children and unhappy lives.

We don't know if Greene's principle that 'Children behave well if they can' is always accurate. But we do know that it is effective. That's enough for us. When parents think this way, conflicts are reduced. Children are happy and develop well, and we adults more often feel that we have succeeded. Everyone wins.

Summary
Children behave well if they can. It is not a matter of willingness. If a child is not behaving, then most likely we have too high demands and expectations regarding his abilities. By thinking through the demands we have on the child in situations that don't go well, we can adjust our expectations and get fewer conflicts in everyday life.

3

Children Always Do What Makes Sense

EMILY

Emily and her father, Stephen, are on their way home from day care. They are in a hurry and so they use the exit that faces the street where Stephen's car is parked, instead of the usual one. Right in front of the door there is a puddle nearly four inches deep and full of water. Just like many other children, Emily loves to splash in water, so she runs straight into the puddle and jumps so that the water splashes everywhere.

'No!' cries Stephen when he sees Emily in the puddle. 'You're not wearing your boots! How many times do I have to tell you not to jump in puddles when you're not wearing your boots?'

UNDERSTANDABLE ACTIONS

Most of us try to do what makes the most sense in the situation in which we happen to be. There are many examples of this. Regardless of the speed limit shown on traffic signs, for example, we tend to drive more slowly on narrow roads than on broader ones – and even slower if the road has many curves. Slowing down when the road gets narrower is the most logical thing to do. In the same way, it is a completely logical and understandable action for a preschool child to jump into an inviting puddle. To choose anything else requires an active impulse control.

This is not about understanding but about what we do when we're not really thinking about it. Parents often think that the best way to increase good behaviour for children is to talk to them. We don't think so. 'Surely you must understand that...' is not a way forward when a child doesn't have the ability to calculate cause and effect in complex situations, as in the case with Emily and the puddle. This is an ability that develops over time and isn't fully developed until about the age of 10 years. Up to a fifth of the population lacks this ability throughout life, and we all lose it when we are stressed.

A great deal of conflict arises in situations where both parents and children are stressed and unable to foresee the consequences of their actions. In such situations we obviously can't use strategies that place demands on the very abilities that children are lacking.

INCOMPREHENSIBLE RULES

One of the most common reasons for conflict between parents and their children is that children don't obey the parents' rules. When we discuss this with parents, most of them think it's obvious that their children must obey the rules. If a problem arises, then the first action taken is often to introduce yet another rule. We have asked these parents if they always obey all the rules of society. It turns out that they do not. We humans follow the rules that make sense. We find it difficult to obey meaningless rules.

A good example of this is the common rule that we shouldn't wear a hat or cap indoors. Adults born before 1975 think that this is a fully understandable rule. Teenagers don't agree. Another common rule is that you have to taste everything. For some children, this is sheer torture. They know that broccoli tastes horrible, but they still have to taste it. A third example is that children must remain at the table until everyone has finished eating. In some families, this causes a lot of conflicts.

As parents, it is important for us to understand that when children don't obey the rules, it almost always comes down to the rules not making sense. It doesn't make sense for children to take off their headwear when they go inside, not when the hat is an expression of their identity. None of us removes our identity just because we happen to be indoors. Nor does it make sense to be forced to taste horrible things or to have to sit at the table and argue when it would be much more fun to be someplace else.

If we require our children to be cap-free indoors, to remain at the table until everyone has finished eating and to taste everything, then we're going to have to remind and nag every day, at least with some children. And this has a cost. Children will start to think that we are idiots who make up meaningless rules – and this undercuts the trust and the confidence in us that they need to feel in order to have a good life.

SHORTCUTS TO SENSE

The principle that we do what makes sense can be applied in many settings. The more meaningful we can make a situation, the easier it becomes for children to do what is expected of them.

If we are going to work with meaningfulness and making sense in everyday life, then there are some shortcuts available. The simplest shortcut is to modify the physical environment.

In certain environments we behave the right way because it makes sense to do so; in others we behave badly because the environment invites us to do so. Children who fight with each other a lot will fight less often if they have their own rooms than if they have to share a room. Assigned seats in the car usually reduce conflict. Sometimes it is the small physical details that make the difference between peace and chaos.

That's why it's always a good idea to start with the physical parameters at home. Calm colours, rooms with quiet acoustics, and hinges that allow cupboard doors, for example, to close quietly instead of being slammed shut – all contribute to a restful environment and create peace and quiet. A noisy environment, with many audible and visible impressions, leads to a more conflict-filled everyday life. Such a simple thing as turning off the stove fan before sitting down to eat can mean that the family's stress level is reduced and conflict at the dinner table is avoided.

Another shortcut to make children do right at home is to help them make their day predictable. Many children have no problem getting the day to pass in a peaceful manner if they have an overview of what they are going to do and for how long. A plan for the day hanging in a visible location for children can significantly reduce conflict. It can be a simple chart of what is going to happen during the day, either illustrated or written (if the child can read), or small drawings on Post-it notes. Crossing out activities once they have been completed further improves the overview. For most children, a day plan is only needed for limited periods of time, or when things are not as usual, but some children can benefit from having one every day.

It can be difficult to get an overview of spare time. For some children, a predetermined and meaningful activity is better than just doing nothing. It increases their ability to understand the day. If they have trouble coming up with an activity on their own, they might need help with concrete suggestions, such as colouring or building, or even playing on the computer or watching a movie.

As we have said before, children are different and have different abilities. This also affects their actions. What makes the most sense for one child can be unimaginable for another, since they have differing abilities.

Summary
Children always do what makes sense in any situation. We can therefore better understand children's fighting if we try to understand how a certain behaviour makes sense to them in a certain situation – why they are acting the way they are. If we want to change children's behaviour, we must change the conditions so that the desired behaviour becomes the most meaningful way to act for the child.

4

The One Who Takes Responsibility Can Make a Difference

JACK AND HARRY

Jack and Harry are in the store shopping with their mother, Debbie. It's Thursday evening, the time is six o'clock and the boys are tired and hungry after a long day. 'I want a hot dog!' whines Jack as he points to the hot-dog vendor outside the store. 'Yes! A hot dog!' says Harry, lighting up.

'Sure, we can have a hot dog while we wait for the bus', replies Debbie while she gathers the last few items and goes towards the line at the cash register. In the meantime Harry catches sight of the comics and runs off to look at them. Jack clings to Debbie. 'I want sweets', he says. Debbie replies that they eat sweets on Saturdays, and says loudly to Harry that he should come and stand in line properly. Harry comes running and in his hurry he accidentally bumps Jack with his elbow. Jack gets mad and shoves Harry hard on the shoulder. Harry responds by pushing Jack away.

'He hit me!' wails Jack. 'I did not, he's just telling lies!' says Harry angrily. Debbie, who has started to put her items on the counter, has suddenly had enough. 'If we're going to have this much fighting, then there aren't going to be any hot dogs', she snarls. Jack starts to cry and Harry turns quiet and sulky. 'No hot dogs', repeats Debbie. She pays the cashier and sharply tells the boys to come along. On the way to the bus stop, she explains to them several times that they really can't behave like babies in the store: they have to get along.

WHOSE RESPONSIBILITY IS IT?

The principle 'The one who takes responsibility can make a difference' was formulated by the psychologist Bernhard Weiner. It spread very widely within occupational psychology, with concepts such as 'Influencing one's own work environment' – which was found to reduce sick leave and improve well-being at workplaces.

In pedagogical contexts, the psychologist Dave Dagnan has taken Weiner's ideas the furthest. In his studies, he has looked at what happens when one assumes that someone is being violent on purpose, as compared with assuming that he is doing his best but not succeeding. It turns out that if people think others are able to control their behaviour and choose to be difficult, then there will be more conflict.

In the example with Jack and Harry, things will get very difficult if Debbie thinks she is doing a good thing by telling Jack and Harry that they can't have hot dogs. Maybe she thinks they will behave better next time they are in the store, but the chances of that happening are small. Instead of taking responsibility herself for changing the situation, she acts on the assumption that it is Jack and Harry who should change their behaviour. So if they fight next time as well, Debbie will be at a loss as to what she should do.

Every time we manage a situation by placing the responsibility for it on the child, we make ourselves powerless. Choosing powerlessness is not the right way to go if you want to reduce conflict.

If we as parents think that it is the children who are responsible for their behaviour in situations like the one with Jack and Harry, then there will be consequences. To begin with, we will experience many similar situations in the future. We will also feel the powerlessness that comes from not being able to influence the children's behaviour. This means that we might end up each day dreading how badly things may go. It may get so bad that it depends on the children whether we have a good day or not. Having things this way will without doubt lead to stress and conflict at home, between parents and children, between siblings and between parents. It will have negative effects on the whole family.

In the situation with Harry and Jack, Debbie needed to decide that the children were doing their best, but that it was difficult for them to stay calm in the store after a long day. With that insight, she would have gained the ability to influence the situation and, in the long run, her own well-being. This would have meant a calmer everyday life and a better atmosphere for everyone involved. And a calm and secure everyday life is good for children's development.

PUNISHMENT AND CONSEQUENCES

When discussing situations like the one with Jack and Harry, parents often feel provoked by our methods. They may say: 'Should children really be allowed to act and speak that way? Should there not be consequences?'

That is an interesting question. First, surely no one thinks that it is OK for Jack and Harry to fight in the store – least of all Jack and Harry. But in a difficult situation, they are doing their best, and it doesn't turn out very well.

A situation is what it is. As parents we have to relate to the immediate situation and try to handle it. The next question is what we can do to reduce the risk of it happening again. At this stage many parents will no doubt start thinking about consequences. Most of us adults think that if children experience a negative consequence after behaving in an undesirable way, then the behaviour will be reduced, because that is how we think it works for us. That's why Jack and Harry don't get any hot dogs.

The concept of consequences has been debated by psychologists, sociologists and scholars for many years. There is a lot of disagreement on the subject, but one factor of interest has emerged: if a child perceives a consequence as a punishment, then the risk increases that things will go wrong again in a similar situation. In other words, it is not so much about what actually happens, but how the child perceives it. Things that happen by accident, like a chair falling over when someone swings on it, are seldom perceived as punishment. But not getting a hot dog because you've been fighting with your brother usually is. And then the risk increases that there will be trouble next time you're in the store, because the consequences that we humans remember and feel have been helpful for us are not the ones we perceived as punishments.

How being punished usually results in a feeling of being unfairly treated

For parents, this should not come as a surprise. Children often say: 'What? It wasn't just me!' when we punish them. To feel unfairly treated by one's parents damages the parent–child relationship – the relationship that is the most important one in the child's life (and hopefully also in our lives). In other words, our parental capital is diminished when we punish.

How punishment increases the very behaviour we are punishing

This is true both on the societal and the individual level. It is the reason why first offenders are often given conditional sentences. An unconditional sentence for a first conviction results in a 150% higher recurrence rate compared with a conditional one. The same thing applies in the family. Every time we punish our children's behaviour, the way Debbie does above, the risk for conflict will increase, not decrease.

How punishment can legitimise children's wrongdoing

Research by the American economists Uri Gneezy and Aldo Rustichini has shown that if fines are imposed for those who pick up their children late from preschool, the number of children remaining at closing time doubles. The reason is that the punishment takes away the bad conscience. Children too are sometimes ready to pay the price of a punishment for doing something they are not allowed to do. Then they don't need to have a bad conscience anymore. We see the same mechanism at work with rewards: if a child doesn't want the offered reward, then he doesn't need to do the right thing. And he doesn't get a bad conscience if he does the wrong thing.

Why we have differing tendencies to punish

This phenomenon is sometimes called the de Quervain effect, after the Swiss neurophysiologist Dominique de Quervain. Together with some colleagues (de Quervain *et al.* 2004), he researched two questions: if there are differences in people who punish, and why they do it. They discovered that different people have differing tendencies to punish, and that you can predict who will have a greater tendency to punish by measuring activity in the brain's reward centre.

The greater the level of activity, the greater the tendency to punish. But the most interesting discovery was that we humans gain a personal sense of reward when we punish someone. It simply feels good! Even if we ourselves actually lose out by punishing, we still get a sense of competence and justice – simply put, a kick.

Researchers have speculated about why this is so. One of these theorists is the anthropologist Robert Boyd. He thinks that, in prehistoric times, those who got rid of people who were causing harm to the flock or the village – by throwing them out before they could cause too much harm – survived better than those who did not. That's why we have developed this reward effect when we punish others. That's why we remove our children from group activities when they do something wrong, order them up to their room and threaten that they will not be allowed to go next time. We change our minds and tell them they can't have a hot dog – even though it increases the risk for conflict. But in families this becomes a problem. We cannot make use of an evolutionary mechanism focused on group survival every time a child acts out. It costs too much in parental capital.

The key question

The question is not whether we should allow, or not allow, our children to say or do things a certain way in a certain situation. The question is how we can make sure that the children don't do the same thing next time in a similar situation. And that brings us back to Chapter 2, 'Children Behave Well If They Can'. What was the breaking point in the situation with Jack and Harry that made it unmanageable for them? What could their mother have done to change the conditions so that things would go better the next time they went shopping? Creating rules about acceptable behaviour would have been meaningless; Jack and Harry wouldn't be able to follow them in any case. It's not rules we need, but rather situations that work.

REWARDS

Since punishment and rewards are two sides of the same coin, we also want to touch on rewards here. Rewards also place responsibility on children.

JULIAN

Julian is 15 years old. He has difficulty getting out of bed in the mornings. His parents leave early for work, so it's up to him to make sure that he gets up and goes to school. About three times a week he arrives a half-hour late. Both the school and his parents consider this to be a problem. Discussions are held and together they come up with a solution: Every time Julian comes to school on time, he gets a smiley. When he has collected five smileys, he gets a ticket to the cinema from his parents. Everyone thinks this is a good solution – the school, Julian and Julian's parents.

The first week goes well. Julian is in school on time every morning. On Saturday he goes to the cinema. The second week goes just as well. Julian goes to the cinema again on Saturday. Then Monday comes.

When Julian doesn't arrive at school, not at nine, nor ten, nor eleven, his teacher phones him and asks: 'Aren't you coming today?' Julian replies: 'No, I think I'll take the day off today.' 'What about tomorrow then?' the teacher continues. Julian says: 'We'll see.' 'But then there will be no cinema ticket for the weekend', says the teacher. Julian answers calmly: 'No, but that doesn't matter, because there aren't any good films this weekend.'

The problem with a token economy like this is that it places the responsibility on Julian, on the child. And Julian willingly accepts that responsibility. But not in the way the school and parents expected. When Julian is prepared to pay the cost of not going to school, he chooses to stay at home. This is a true story. In Julian's case, this led to a tenfold increase in his absences. The reason is that rewards, just like punishments, can legitimise the feeling that it is OK to do wrong. In our experience, a token economy can have the result that the very behaviour we want to see increase actually becomes less frequent than before we started to offer rewards – the exact opposite of what we want to achieve.

Rewards also have a tendency to affect us humans in such a way that we start doing things in order to get a reward, instead of doing them because we want to do them, or realise that we ought to do them.

Some side effects of token economies
The inflation effect

All token economies involve negotiation. Parents usually make an estimate of how little reward can be offered to gain the desired behaviour. If the child accepts the reward, then it works. But all negotiations imply that, after a while, the child can try to negotiate for a bigger reward. This often happens over time. There is inflation in the economy and children require greater and greater rewards for the same behaviour.

The diminishing-satisfaction effect

When you get your first pay cheque, it's a fantastic feeling. Every subsequent time you receive your pay during the first year of work, that feeling is diminished. After a few years, you're mostly just relieved that the pay arrives at all. The joy in receiving a reward for work done diminishes over time.

Maybe because when you're young, you're not sure that you are worthy of the pay. As they become more experienced, most people feel that they deserve more. We see the same effect when rewards are an integral part of a family's everyday life. After a few years, inflation has increased to the point where it costs a video game per week just to get everyday life to function. But the reward doesn't bring joy anymore, since the children feel that they deserve it. It's very sad to see a 13-year-old who doesn't get any joy from receiving a reward.

The punishment effect

In token economies it is often described as a reward when children receive a star if, for example, they arrive on time. When they have earned 10 stars, they can exchange them for an activity or something similar. But if they arrive late, and therefore don't get a star, they often perceive this as a punishment – even if the parents only see it as a missed reward. Sometimes conflicts also arise when the child feels that he didn't do wrong on purpose. When an unpaid reward is perceived as punishment, then the token economy won't work as intended – because, as mentioned above, punishment does not have the positive effect that many of us think it does.

The opposition effect

A reward is, at its core, part of a power relationship. It is the parents who decide what should be rewarded and when the children have earned the reward. This places the parents in a relationship of opposition to the children. Some psychologists try to avoid this by recommending that the rewards be discussed with children and that they themselves be allowed to suggest rewards and when they are to be given out. This is better, but in most cases it is still the parents who decide.

The behaviour-reducing effect

The token economy is built on the idea that motivation for the behaviour we are rewarding will increase, so that we can phase out the reward after a while. This is not the case. American psychologist Edward Deci and his research group have shown, in many studies, that behaviour that is rewarded diminishes when the reward disappears. It actually diminishes to levels that are lower than before we started offering the reward. This means that we need to be careful when we use rewards. An occasional reward may be effective when, for example, a child has to go to the dentist and is scared, but don't use rewards for doing homework or similar everyday activities, because then the homework done will be reduced in the long run, when we phase out the token economy. And let's be honest: How many adults would go to work if the salary was phased out?

The someone-has-to-win effect

A relationship of opposition means that someone always has to win – either the parents or the children. At the beginning parents take it for granted that they will be the winners, but this is often opposed by children. This is not so strange. No one wants to lose. But it means that the relationship between parents and children suffers. This book works on the assumption that it is better to cooperate with children than to fight with them. And so the token economy becomes a problem. It works against cooperation because of the built-in power structure.

Use rewards with care

We meet a great many parents of children who act out that have gone to various courses in order to learn how to manage their children – perhaps through social welfare services, or child and youth psychiatry. Most of these courses have included rewards and token economies of various kinds, and they often haven't worked. We also meet professionals who don't teach about token economies, even though they are meant to be part of the course they are offering, because they know that they don't work. It is simply much too difficult to succeed. The basic reason for all the side effects of token economies is that they place the responsibility on the child – which means the parents lose the possibility to make a difference, because only the one who takes responsibility can make a difference.

Giving your 2-year-old a Kinder Egg after cutting her hair is not a problem in itself. Rewards have their place in rare but important situations. But receiving a Kinder Egg for not fighting is meaningless and will, unfortunately, not work in the long run. It has too many side effects.

'HITTING THE SKILL CEILING'

We parents are quite good at taking responsibility when we have a good method, a good way to handle a situation. When we know what to do and what works, we are happy to do it. But sometimes we end up in situations where we don't have a functioning method or the appropriate skill. We can't get any further with the method we are using. We can call this 'hitting the skill ceiling'.

This often happens in situations where something that usually works suddenly doesn't work. For example, many parents have a rule that children must taste all food that is served. As long as the children taste the food, perhaps with the help of a little persuasion or nagging, we feel that the method works well. But then one day the child flatly refuses. We try with everything we have, but nothing helps.

Our method, which was based on persistence, no longer works. Then there is a risk that we will say: 'If you don't taste everything, there'll be no dessert.'

When parents hit the skill ceiling in this manner, then we have a tendency to immediately place the responsibility on children by punishing them (with arguments such as 'Then maybe they'll learn', or 'They must take responsibility') or by shouting, screaming and scolding. Perhaps we sometimes think: *They have to behave, and if they don't understand that the first time I say it, then I'll have to say it again, but louder, so that they do understand!*

Another common reaction is to try to avoid responsibility by demanding that the child behave. We have talks with them about how they should behave. But if our only method is to talk to children about what they should do, it is probably because we don't know what *we* should do. If our method, persistence, doesn't work any longer, then we have to find a better method – one that works – or possibly change the goal. (Maybe it's not that important to taste everything.) Above all, we have to find a method that places the responsibility on ourselves, because every time we try to get our children to take responsibility and fail, we ourselves also lose the possibility of succeeding.

We often meet parents who disagree about how to tackle their children when they act out. They often place responsibility for the child's behaviour on the other parent. They think the other parent's method is bad. Sometimes we even come across psychologists and others who think that the reason children act out is that the parents are not in agreement about how to manage them. This is not why children act out in our experience, however. If children act out, it's most likely the case that neither parent has a method that works.

If we are to succeed as parents, then we have to change our methods until they actually work. We must not stop trying, because then we are really letting our children down. That children act out doesn't diminish our responsibility as parents, but rather increases it. So if we are to succeed, we have to recognise when we have reached the skill ceiling. This is perhaps one of the most important things we need to know as parents: To understand when things have gone wrong, so that we have the possibility to change. We can develop new skills and better methods.

'HOW MANY TIMES MUST I TELL YOU…?'

'Insanity is doing the same thing over and over again and expecting a different result'. This quotation is ascribed, probably incorrectly, to Albert Einstein. But regardless of who said it, one has to agree.

One way of recognizing when we reach the skill ceiling is to count. Have we tried this several times already? Did it work before? If not, should we then really try it again?

The skill ceiling is dangerous. Every time we start laying all the responsibility for children's behaviour on the children themselves, we lose the possibility to make a difference. This means that we end up powerless, stressed and burned out. Instead, we have to make use of methods that work. We have to know what works for our specific child in a given situation and, not least, evaluate whether what we are doing is having good effect; in other words, whether the child is managing the situation with the help of our method. If, for example, we have had a talk with the child about what he should do and it hasn't helped, then it probably isn't the child's fault. It's probably we who have used a method that places too high expectations on the child's abilities.

Should we then drop all expectations and demands on our children? Yes and no. Changing methods can sometimes mean that we have to forget about certain activities or demands. But most often it is enough to change the way in which we make the demands. Jack and Harry would probably have fought less if Debbie had given them a hot dog each before they went into the store. Julian might have managed to get to school on time if one of his parents had been at home with him each morning.

The trick in reaching the desired goal is to make our demands of our children in a new and different way. We have to use a different method that doesn't place too high demands on the child's abilities. Then we can finally succeed. We will get back to this particular aspect in Chapter 10.

BUT SHOULD CHILDREN NOT LEARN TO TAKE RESPONSIBILITY THEMSELVES?

Yes, of course. This is perhaps the core of the job of being a parent. Our children should grow up into independent and responsible adults. The method we use is to train them to take responsibility. Children learn by succeeding. Every time a child is able to take responsibility for himself, he should be given the chance to do so – initially with support in the form of our being available in the background, ready to step in if necessary, and later by believing in the child's abilities and allowing him to try to manage on his own, even if it's difficult. However, if a child does not succeed in taking responsibility, then we have to take it back. So we need to always have an invisible safety net under our children. We are responsible for teaching children to take responsibility themselves, and also for taking back the responsibility when children don't succeed – because, as we shall see in the next chapter, children don't learn anything from failure.

Summary

By accepting responsibility we create the possibility to influence our situation. If we think that it is children who should solve the problems we experience, then we lose the possibility to make a difference and we become powerless. When we deal with conflict situations we must therefore avoid methods that put the responsibility elsewhere than on ourselves. We should avoid punishments, consequences, rewards and reprimands when we want to influence our children's behaviour. In order to achieve change, we have to use methods that allow children to succeed.

REFERENCE

de Quervain, D.J.F., Fischbacher, U., Treyer, V., Schellhammer M. *et al.* (2004) 'The neural basis of altruistic punishment.' *Science 305*, 1254–1258.

5

Children Learn Nothing from Failure

GRACE

Grace plays the violin. She has played since she was 7 years old. At the age of 10 years she plays reasonably well. She practises a little every day and has 25 minutes of instruction every week. On Christmas Eve she wants to play Christmas carols at home. Her parents listen patiently. She's not entirely sure of the notes. The rhythm is a little off and she doesn't remember everything. Her brother Charlie, who is 12 years old, says: 'Enough already! It sounds terrible!' Grace answers: 'I'm only 10 years old. Of course it's not perfect.'

AMIR

Amir is 1 year old. In the past few months he has been practising walking beside the furniture. Sometimes he falls, but that doesn't put him off. Today he sees his mother a bit further out on the floor, and suddenly he walks three steps towards her before falling over. She is thrilled and cries: 'He walked three steps on his own! His first steps!'

For the rest of the afternoon, she sits in the middle of the floor and tries to get Amir to walk to her again. He often falls, but he gets more and more confident every time he succeeds. It's a good day.

DO WE LEARN FROM SUCCESS OR FAILURE?

Both Grace and Amir in the examples above fail repeatedly. Grace doesn't play all that well. She can hear it herself, but she thinks it's obvious that her playing is not going to be perfect. She's only 10 years old! Amir lets go of the furniture even though he fell over last time he did so.

In both these situations the point is that Grace and Amir don't have a problem with failure. That's what they are used to. If they had learned from failure, then they would both have stopped – Grace from playing the violin and Amir from trying to walk.

The principle 'Children learn nothing from failure' is based on research by neuropsychologist Anna van Duijvenvoorde and her colleagues in the Netherlands. van Duijvenvoorde was interested in finding out whether we humans learn from success or failure. She used a magnetic resonance imaging camera which measures brain activity during various activities.

The experiment was simple: Each subject was given a number of problems to solve in about 15 minutes. They were not told how to solve them. If they solved a problem well, they received praise of the type: 'That was right'. When it went wrong they were told: 'Now it was wrong'.

The results were completely unexpected. When people over 15 years old were told 'Now it was wrong', brain activity increased in the areas of the brain that we know have to do with learning. If the same people were told 'Now it was right', brain activity in the same areas instead dropped a great deal. When the same experiment was done with children under

11 years old, the opposite results were seen. When they were told they were right, activity increased in the areas of the brain that have to do with learning. When they were told they were wrong, the activity decreased.

Van Duijvenvoorde interprets this increase in activity in the brain as an expression of learning. The conclusion she draws is that people over 15 years old learn from failure, whereas children under 11 years old learn from success. Between the ages of 11 and 15 years, it varies a little from child to child, which she takes to mean that children of this age are in the process of developing from learning by success to learning by failure.

The theory builds on the principle that we learn by deviation from the norm. All children fail all the time when they are small. As they grow older, though, they become more and more skilful at many things, and somewhere before the age of 15 years, most children start to succeed more often than they fail.

Small children are surprised when they succeed, while as adults we are surprised when we fail. And somewhere between being a child and an adult we go from learning from success to learning from failure. This is one of the reasons why many children stop doing a sport or playing a musical instrument around the age of 13 to 15 years. They suddenly discover that they are not good at it. Only those who are good carry on.

This means that the opposite also applies: that as normal and well-functioning adults we are not surprised when someone tells us that we are good at something, whereas small children are not the least surprised when something goes wrong. Small children can repeat the same mistake over and over again – and then just keep going – because they don't expect to get it right.

Unfortunately, we parents often act from our own experience. This means that we perhaps think our children will learn something from their mistakes. And when they don't, we risk hitting the skill ceiling, as discussed in the previous chapter.

WHY REPRIMANDS DON'T WORK

If we are to take Anna van Duijvenvoorde's research seriously, then we who have children under 15 years of age must refrain from reprimanding them, because most likely it has no effect. On the other hand, it may be a good idea if we instead tell them what to do next time in order to succeed. And we should definitely let them know when they are successful, preferably by praising their efforts: 'You worked hard. And the result was good, too. It all turned out great!'

Even if children are not completely successful, we can still use this knowledge. We can give praise for the things that worked, and that we know are needed in order for them to reach final success. In this way we help them to discover and remember what they need to do to get it right the next time.

The fact that children don't learn from failure – but rather from success – means that the usual protest, 'If we don't tell them they've done wrong, they won't learn anything', becomes meaningless. If as parents we instead adjust our daily routines to match the child's abilities, then they will succeed, and so they will also learn. Thereafter we can gradually increase our demands in line with their increasing ability. This may also mean that, in the long run, they will become so used to succeeding that they will begin to learn from failure.

ABOUT PRACTICE

That children don't learn from failure does not mean that they don't learn from practising. They do. Grace learns to play the violin by playing the violin. Amir learns to walk by walking. But as parents we sometimes think that we can speed up the learning process through reprimands, punishments and consequences. We think that children learn not to do something just because it doesn't go well or because it has negative consequences. But if this had been the case, then Grace would have stopped playing the violin a long time ago; after all, she has been playing for several years and it still doesn't sound very good. And Amir would have given up learning to walk, because at the age of 1 year he has practised walking for a quarter of his life without success. And you who are reading this would probably never have learned to read. You would have quit after a couple of weeks of trying.

To learn through practice, you have to be able to cope with failure – and children can. They don't give up just because it's not going so well. And that is exactly why they don't learn from negative consequences or reprimands. In other words, learning from failure and coping with failure are different things.

HOW THOSE USED TO FAILURE
LEARN FROM SUCCESS

Whether a child or a youth learns from success or failure doesn't really depend on their age. It depends on how often the child succeeds in everyday life. Some children find it very easy to live up to the demands of their surroundings, and so succeed for the most part. They will therefore transition to learning from the things that don't go so well at an early stage, perhaps as early as 11 years of age. But most children start to succeed more often than they fail somewhere between the ages of 13 and 15 years. That's when they start to learn more from failure than from success.

Then there are a few children who fail more often than others, for example by fighting a lot. Some of them will be used to failing, even though they are 15 years of age or older. Not until they begin to succeed more often than they fail can they begin to learn from their mistakes.

If we have well-functioning youths over the age of 15 years, we can correct them by calmly explaining what went wrong. But only if it is an exception that things go wrong. For young people who continue to fail, correction will not have any effect whatsoever. Only youths who succeed more than they fail can benefit from it.

Thus, the more often children or young people fail, the less they will learn from it. This means that we can disregard statements such as: 'If we make pedagogic adjustments, then the child won't learn anything' and 'How will he manage in the real world if we make too many adjustments?' Failing repeatedly does not mean that the child will manage better as an adult.

Children who are used to failure first have to succeed a lot – until they are really used to succeeding. Only then can they learn from failure. In practice, this means that our most important job as parents is always to help our children succeed. And that is actually the best thing there is!

Summary

Most adults learn something every time they fail. That is why we usually only make the same mistake a few times. But children can make the same mistake over and over again without it leading to their stopping the activity at which they are failing. Instead, they learn when they succeed. The more often a child fails, the less they learn from it. This is why reprimands and punishments don't work.

6

You Need Self-control to Cooperate with Others

LILY

Lily is 5 years old and a sensitive child. When it's time for an evening snack she says: 'May I have some juice?' Her father, John, answers that there is fruit juice if she wants it. Then Lily starts to cry. 'You don't understand what I'm saying! I'm not talking about fruit juice! Fruit juice is not juice! You don't understand anything!'

John tries to explain that he offered her fruit juice because the normal juice is finished, not because he didn't understand her question, but Lily is much too upset to listen. She can't stop crying or choose something else to drink.

After a little while she agrees to sit on John's lap. He manages to persuade her to eat some cereal and milk, and he jokes with her so that the crying stops. But it takes a long time to eat, and for the rest of the evening Lily is tired and she doesn't have the energy to put on her own pyjamas like she usually does. When John brings out the toothbrush with Lily's favourite toothpaste, she goes and hides under the bed.

CHILDREN IN AFFECT

The principle 'You need self-control to cooperate with others' is easy to understand if you think about it. As parents, we often think we can tell our children to calm down when they are stressed and upset, when they are in affect. But that's not how children work. A child in affect is a child who can't think normally and who acts impulsively to a greater degree than otherwise. Reasoning with the child in this situation doesn't usually produce any results; nor does raising one's voice have the desired effect.

If we consider the situation with Lily in the light of what we have discussed so far, then we can see that she is unable to control her feelings when her father tells her that she can't have juice. She does the thing that is most meaningful in the situation, seen from her agitated perspective: she cries. Her father is asking too much of her ability to handle unexpected changes and to regulate her affect. Lily can't just 'calm down' – her adrenaline level is simply too high.

That our children cooperate actually means that of their own free will, they give up some of their self-control to us parents – by doing what we ask them to do. This they can do only when they have control over themselves.

THE OUTBURST-OF-AFFECT MODEL

In many situations we, as parents, have to handle our children's anger and lack of self-control. Sometimes we have to act immediately when something happens, in order to protect a sibling or other child. At other times it's enough to wait for a while, as in the situation above, where Lily needed time to calm down before she could curl up on John's lap. The important thing, however, is to understand what is happening in situations where conflict arises or where children react strongly – and to know what we can do in the different stages of the situation.

In 1983, researchers Stephen Kaplan and Eugenie Wheeler (Kaplan and Wheeler 1983) created a basic model of the various phases in an emotional storm, an outburst of affect, which has since been presented in countless versions. Figure 6.1 shows our version of their model.

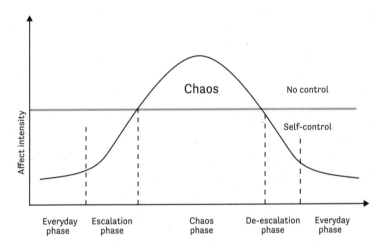

Figure 6.1 The outburst-of-affect model (from Elvén 2010)

The *vertical axis* in Figure 6.1 shows the strength of emotion, and the *horizontal axis* shows time. The *curve* shows what the progression of affect can look like in a conflict or chaos situation. The *line* in the middle of the graph shows how much affect the person can tolerate.

Newborn babies can't tolerate very much. They lose control every time they get hungry. So, for them, this line lies very low down in the model. With age, they get better and better at handling both hunger and affect, and the line moves upward. This we call maturing. As adults we can handle most situations and so the line lies above the curve for most of us.

But for some children the line remains noticeably lower than for most others in their age group. It means that they lose control of themselves more often than others do. They have greater difficulty than others in regulating their affect.

The model's different fields

There are five fields in the model, describing five different phases. In the first, the everyday phase, the level of affect is low. The child is just taking it easy or is in a situation that is working well. Then a trigger factor appears, an affect trigger. In Lily's case, it's that her father offers her fruit juice instead of normal juice. In the next phase, the escalation phase, it is still possible to communicate with the child. Communication is not as good as in the everyday phase, but there is still a chance of finding a way to calm the child. In this phase, children usually look for strategies to solve the situation, which Lily does by talking and trying to influence her father. Occasionally the situation will escalate to the chaos phase, in which case the child is beyond reach and no longer acts strategically. But after a while (because it always passes), the child gradually calms down (the de-escalation phase) and eventually returns to the everyday phase.

The skidding car

To better explain what the outburst-of-affect model teaches us about parenting, we can do a thought experiment.

Let's imagine we are driving to work. It's a lovely spring day. Driving conditions are good and we drive as usual. We obviously have to pay attention to the traffic, but steering, turning and braking all work just fine. Our usual methods of making demands of our vehicle are working well.

Further along, the road gets a little icy. Perhaps we test the brakes and notice that we need to adjust our driving. So we keep a greater distance to other cars, brake more softly, drive more slowly. Perhaps we even change our planned route in order to avoid a particularly risky section of the road. After all, we have driven this way many times before. We know where the most dangerous places are and when it's not worth the risk to drive there.

Driving a car under good conditions is like making simple demands in everyday life. Children have full self-control and can manage to do what we ask of them. We can think of the demand as a kind of test braking. It often goes well.

But sometimes the demand makes affect start to rise. In some children this is easy to see, whereas others only give subtle indications – perhaps a particular tone of voice or slightly jerky movements. Parents of children who only show subtle signs in the escalation phase often describe it as if the children 'explode like lightning from a clear sky'. More often it is a case of the parents having missed the signals that the child is in the escalation phase. It is like driving conditions changing without you being able to see it.

But many children give very clear signals. They may start crying, like Lily, or they say no, loud and clear. But they rarely break down completely in one go.

The escalation phase is like the slipperiness that we notice, but that doesn't cause the car to skid. Whereas we were just now driving along without thinking, we suddenly have to slow down and be more alert. In the same way, we need to adjust our methods in both the escalation and the de-escalation phases so that our behaviour doesn't drive the child's affect upwards, towards the chaos phase.

We will get the best cooperation, of course, in the everyday phase, when children are fully in control of themselves. In the escalation and the de-escalation phases, it is more difficult but still possible. But it requires us to adjust quite a lot just then.

So we keep driving down the road. But we have completely misjudged the road conditions. Suddenly the car skids violently. Now we are no longer in control of the car: we can neither steer nor brake. Actually, braking or steering to the side would probably be about the worst thing we could do.

In a skid to the right, the best thing to do is something that feels completely wrong: to disengage the gear and steer to the right – steering with the skid, not against it. Then it will be as short as possible, since we will not cause new skids by emerging from the first one with our wheels pointing in the wrong direction.

The chaos phase is like a major skid. We cannot steer either a child or a car that is unsteerable. But by disengaging the gear (temporarily dropping a demand until the child is able to control himself) and steering with the skid (supporting the child's efforts to regain self-control), we can make the chaos phase as short as possible. In addition, we reduce the risk of injury, because a violent outburst can be dangerous, both for the child and for us parents.

After skidding with the car, we usually drive more carefully for a while. That is a good thing to do, because there is considerable risk that the road will continue to be slippery for some distance. We are not yet back in the everyday phase, driving on good roads. We are in the de-escalation phase and still need to be careful.

Adjusting methods to the level of affect

Most children that have reached a certain age manage to stay in control of themselves even though their parents sometimes make mistakes. This is one reason why normal methods of upbringing, which research has shown to be ineffective, still seem to work. For most children, they don't make the situation much worse. But some children have much greater difficulty than others in retaining control, just as some makes of cars skid more easily than others. Some vehicles simply require a more careful style of driving. And some children require better methods.

A child behaves differently in the different phases, and as parents we must use different methods in the different phases if we are to resolve the situation in a good way. We will discuss this in the coming chapters and also in the second part of the book. For now, the most important thing to know is that we can only cooperate with our children when they are below the line in the outburst-of-affect model. If their level of affect rises over the line, then there is no possibility of establishing communication at all.

Children usually cooperate well in the everyday phase, when they have full self-control. In the escalation and de-escalation phases, it is possible but difficult. One of the reasons for this is that children in these phases are fully preoccupied with trying to retain control. There is a risk that we disturb this process if we try to control children or make demands of abilities that they normally have, such as being able to listen when we speak to them, because practically all abilities are reduced when the affect level rises.

CONTROL, STRUCTURE AND INDEPENDENCE

There are some theories and a lot of research specifically about control and the raising of children. As early as the 1960s, an American research group started looking at various parenting characteristics and what they meant for a child's development. This has been nicely described by psychologist Wendy S. Grolnick.

At one end of Grolnick's control scale are the parents who demand obedience and who use various methods to get their children to act in a certain way. It may be through scolding, punishment, rewards or by giving orders. At the other end of the scale we find the parents who try to encourage their children to think for themselves by asking questions, explaining and involving the children in discussions. It's not that these parents give up control or let the children decide; rather, they create self-control in the children not by demanding obedience, but getting them to think. In the example with Lily, this is what her father does when he explains that there isn't any juice. He does so a little late, but he does it. If he had done it at the start, perhaps Lily would not have lost control.

Another important factor that Grolnick describes is the degree of structure around children. That scale stretches from chaos to very structured. Grolnick describes structure as something that makes it easier for children to know where the boundaries are, what they are going to do and what is expected of them.

Grolnick thinks that, as parents, we should have a good structure so that children's everyday life is predictable, but at the same time focus on supporting them in being independent rather than obedient. So we will not focus on controlling children's behaviour, but rather on creating good conditions for them to be able to do the right thing.

Sometimes we find that psychologists, as well as parents, politicians and others, mix up structure and control. This happens when they talk about the need to set boundaries and be consistent, but this actually means giving reprimands and making use of punishment and consequences.

A functioning structure means that children know what is going to happen, know how things work and choose to do the best thing. This helps making everyday life meaningful, as discussed earlier. Strict control, on the other hand, is when we focus on making sure that children keep within the structure and when we use methods with that purpose. It may be rewards, punishments and reprimands and, worst of all, conditional love – anything to get the child to obey.

A much better alternative to strict control is to create a structure that works, which makes it easier for all concerned to maintain their self-control. Focusing on a functioning structure instead of on control means that we are training children to behave themselves and to manage their everyday life. If this doesn't work, we need to investigate what is wrong with the structure. We shouldn't try to force children to stay within the structure, to obey, because this is simply not very effective.

Grolnick has identified two additional factors, which she calls warmth and involvement. Her research suggests that children who develop best with regard to both scholarly achievement and behaviour have parents who place low value on control and high value on warmth and involvement, while also managing to maintain a good structure around children.

Most parenting courses focus on warmth, love and control, but mix up control and structure into one big mess, with a little focus on structure, and a lot on the consequences when the child doesn't follow the structure. We would have wished that they would focus on how we can increase the child's self-control rather than how we can control the child's behaviour. A better parenting course would focus primarily on warmth and involvement, but also on structure, which means that the child knows what is going to happen, what is acceptable and where the boundaries lie – not on rewards and consequences.

After all, what characteristics do we want our children to have when they grow up? Do we want them to be obedient or independent?

Summary

For our children to be able to cooperate with us, they need to have control over themselves. Cooperation means lending control to someone else. But to be able to do so means that *you* must first have control. So, if as parents we want to increase the level of cooperation with our children, we cannot use methods intended to control them.

REFERENCE

Kaplan, S.G. and Wheeler, E.G. (1983) 'Survival skills for working with potentially violent clients.' *Social Casework* 64, 339–345.

7

We All Do What We Can to Maintain Self-control

OLIVIA

Olivia is 10 years old. She is sitting at the kitchen table colouring when her big brother, Jacob, comes in. He's angry. He says: 'Olivia, was it you who swiped my video game console?' Olivia denies it.

Jacob starts searching the kitchen and, after a while, he looks in Olivia's bag. Olivia exclaims: 'What are you doing in my bag? You have no right to look in there!' Jacob finds a note in the bag and reads out loud: 'Do you want to go out with me? Noah.' 'Who is Noah?' he asks. 'That's none of your business!' shouts Olivia. Then Jacob starts to chant: 'Noah and Olivia, Noah and Olivia.' Olivia throws her crayons at him, runs to her room and locks the door.

DOING ALL WE CAN TO AVOID
LOSING SELF-CONTROL

The principle 'Everyone does what he can to retain self-control' is one with which most of us can identify. Quite simply, we do all we can to avoid losing control. This is not so strange. None of us want to throw furniture around, break windows, scream, fight, bang our head against a wall or defecate in our pants. So we do what we can to avoid ending up in chaos – especially when we are in the escalation phase (see Figure 6.1).

In the example above, Olivia gets so angry that she throws her crayons at Jacob. But she realises that she is losing her self-control. That is why she does something very wise: she runs off to her room and locks the door. In there she has a chance to calm down. If she had stayed with Jacob, she might well have ended up doing worse things than throwing crayons.

We humans have different ways of trying to retain our self-control. Some ways are effective and good strategies; others may be effective, but may not be as well received by those around us. We all use both types. Let's have a look at some examples.

Effective and good strategies for retaining self-control are as follows:

- You can try to get away in difficult situations in order to get a little peace and quiet.

- You can screen yourself off so that you remain in the situation, but in such a way that the difficult part doesn't feel so difficult, for example by avoiding eye contact or hiding under the hood of your sweatshirt.

- You can decide that things will work out in the end and concentrate on that.

- You can do something you are used to doing so that you feel secure.

- You can look to others for support.

Other strategies for retaining self-control include:

- You can refuse.

  Just say no. This is perhaps the simplest method there is – but also the most dangerous. A great many conflicts between children and parents begin with a demand to which the child says no.

- You can lie in order to manage a difficult situation.

  Research by the Canadian psychologist Victoria Talwar has shown that you lie to protect yourself if this is the simplest solution. Normal teenagers and adults usually do this in a sophisticated manner, and the lie is not detected. But quite a lot of children lie quite badly, and we see immediately that they are lying. To lie well requires the ability to figure out what others are thinking, feeling and experiencing. Children under the age of 7 years haven't developed so far in this area and are often quite bad at lying. Some children go on lying badly even when they get older. Parents who complain that their children over 10 years lie a lot have often got it the wrong way round. These children probably lie less often than other children of the same age. It's just that we catch them doing it more often because their ability to figure out how to lie successfully is not very good. We have to take this deficient ability into account with children that we think lie a lot. They are doing their best; it's just not going all that well.

- You can threaten to go away or to hit someone.

- You can run away.

- You can hit out at others so that they keep their distance.

- You can look for social affirmation by using swear words and the like.

As parents, we can easily perceive the latter list of methods as making trouble. When our children use these methods, we can easily get upset and increase the level of conflict a step or two. This unfortunately increases the risk that the child will lose control, which leads to still more conflict. If, instead, we understand that it's a matter of strategic behaviours that children resort to in order to solve a problem, and not to cause trouble, then we increase our chances of keeping the situation calm and safe for everyone involved.

As parents, therefore, we have to try to avoid placing a moral filter on these types of reactions in our children. The behaviour is not wrong in itself, but rather a way of trying to manage a situation without losing self-control. At the time, we should therefore support our children in their efforts to maintain control, for example by giving them space and doing our best to keep ourselves calm. (We will discuss this more in the next chapter.)

If we want to change our children's behaviour, then we also need to find out why the conflict arose – so that we can change the conditions and prevent the behaviour from happening again. It may be as simple as curiously asking children why they acted the way they did, and then discussing with them what we could do to handle things in a better way the next time.

OFFERING AN ALTERNATIVE STRATEGY

The strategies discussed above are about retaining self-control. The very worst thing we can do is to demand that children refrain from using a certain strategy without offering them an alternative. It can be quite effective, for example, to talk to children about what they can do the next time they end up in a similar situation. Then we give them examples of better strategies, which the children probably wouldn't have thought of themselves in any case. On the other hand, saying, 'You can't act like that. Surely you understand that things go badly then' unfortunately doesn't provide enough support for them to actually refrain from acting like that next time, because children always try to retain self-control, but sometimes they use strategies that don't work so well. Then we need to help them find new and better ones.

If we look again at the outburst-of-affect model (see Figure 6.1), we see that the lessons from this chapter imply that all methods used during the escalation phase must have as their ultimate goal that children retain their self-control.

Summary
Children do their best to retain their self-control. A large part of what we as parents see as causing trouble actually consists of strategies that the child is using to retain self-control, in order to be able to cooperate. If we counteract their strategies, it will often result in more conflict.

8

Emotions Are Contagious

TOBY

Toby is 9 months old. He's lying in the baby carriage watching quietly while his mother has coffee with her friend. The friend also has her baby with her in a baby carriage, which is standing next to Toby's carriage. Suddenly the baby wakes up and starts to cry. Toby thinks: *Someone around here is unhappy – and it's probably me*, and so he also starts to cry.

FREYA

Freya is 9 years old. She's watching TV when her mother, Brenda, comes into the living room. Brenda says angrily: 'Are you sitting here watching TV again? You were meant to be cleaning your room. Off you go, lazybones!'

Freya shouts back: 'Lazybones yourself, you stupid old bag.' She runs off and locks herself in her room. Brenda gets angry and runs after her, but by the time she reaches the door it's already locked. She ends up standing outside the door, trying to get Freya to open up by threatening that she won't get her snack if she doesn't. 'I don't care!' shouts Freya. After a while, Brenda gets tired of trying to get Freya to cooperate.

Freya doesn't come out of her room until her father, Thomas, gets home. Later that evening, after Freya has gone to bed, Brenda says to Thomas: 'That damn kid. She always has to argue. I don't know how to get her to do what I tell her to do.' 'It usually goes well if you can just stay calm. As soon as I get angry I'm done for. So I try to simply stay calm', answers Thomas.

MIRROR NEURONS

We humans have many different feelings; some of these are called 'affects'. These are feelings that exist in all cultures and look the same in different people. They include feelings such as anger, surprise and joy. The concept of affect contagion, which describes how feelings are transmitted from person to person, was formulated by the psychologist Silvan Tomkins as early as the 1960s, but only in the 1990s did the neurophysiologist Giacomo Rizzolatti, in Italy, describe how it works. The pattern of activity that a person has in his brain when he does different things is mirrored in other people's brains by what are known as mirror neurons. This means that if someone smiles, then those who see the smile have the same pattern of activity in their brains as if they had smiled themselves – which can lead to them actually doing so!

We humans experience other people's feelings by becoming infected with them. In other words, it's easier to be happy when you are with happy people, and we are made calm by being together with calm people.

Newborn babies have an extreme level of affect contagion. They are greatly affected by the feelings of the people around them. They think that other people's feelings are their own. That is why a baby will cry when another baby cries, like Toby in the example.

At the age of 18 months, most children begin to understand that the feelings they sense are not always their own. Then they can begin to comfort others. By the age of 4 years, children's ability to stay calm when others are stressed is more or less in place – that is, if they are not stressed themselves. Stressed children (and adults) are very much affected by other peoples' feelings.

There are also some differences in how easy it is for children over 4 years to screen themselves off from other people's feelings. Some children are very little affected by others' affects, most children are affected to some degree and certain children are extremely affected by, for example, their parents' feelings, and not least by other children's emotional states. They simply can't screen themselves off from other people's affects.

Toby is sensitive to other people's feelings. This is because he is so young. Freya is also sensitive to other people's feelings. But she is not so young. She belongs to the 10% of all children with whom we as parents fight the most. These 10% are the ones that have the greatest difficulty in screening themselves off from other people's feelings. Freya gets angry when her mother Brenda is angry.

When Brenda is angry, she and Freya make a bad combination. In the example, Brenda's temperament and her tendency to scold Freya affect Freya so much that her ability to handle everyday life is reduced. When Brenda gets angry, Freya reacts strongly. She can't keep calm as well as most other children of her age. She is most content when she has calm people around her, people who are good at regulating their own affect.

OUR REACTIONS INFECT OUR CHILDREN

If we return to the principles discussed in earlier chapters we can conclude that Brenda, because of her personality, places too high demands on Freya's affect-regulation ability. Because she is the mother and Freya the child, she must either change her ways or protect Freya by allowing her to be on her own more, especially when Brenda herself is upset. Brenda has to take the responsibility for Freya's well-being that is necessary for Freya's daily life to function.

This becomes more important if you frequently end up in conflict with your children. The more conflicts parents have with their children, the more determined they often become in both tone of voice and body language. Unfortunately, this has the result that children also become more determined and that the risk for conflict increases. Perhaps the parents also use marked body language, such as requiring eye contact and moving closer to the child in the demand situation. This kind of behaviour increases the affect contagion and, with it, the risk that a conflict will arise.

To diminish the risk for conflict you should do the following:

- Never demand eye contact.

  Parents often require eye contact when we want a child to obey. We do this because, through the eye contact, they can feel how angry or determined we are. But eye contact also increases the affect contagion and usually leads to an escalation of the conflict.

- Never maintain eye contact for longer than 3 seconds in a demand or conflict situation.

  Eye contact that lasts longer than this creates a powerful affect contagion in a positive or a negative direction, but not in the direction we want in our relationship with our children. Psychologist Daniel Stern once said that 30 seconds of eye contact will end in either violence or sex. This is probably not true, but it is most often in that type of situation that we make use of prolonged eye contact.

- Take a step backwards (physically) in demand situations and in potential conflict situations.

  Going closer to a child when making a demand or setting a boundary increases their stress level. By instead taking a step backwards at the same time as you make a demand, the increased stress that the demand leads to is balanced out, with the result that affect contagion is reduced.

- You can also take a step backwards mentally.

  Chapter 15 of this book is about using a gentle approach. It could, for example, be a matter of saying: 'You're going to bed now. Which pyjamas do you want to wear?' By giving the child a choice (of pyjamas) you move the focus away from the demand and create a feeling of autonomy, which makes it easier for the child to cooperate.

- Sit down if the child is anxious, or lean against a wall.

  Take a deep breath and relax your shoulders. A calm body is as infectious as a tense one, but with calmness. And the goal, of course, is for the child to be calm.

- Stand with your body slightly turned away and not directly facing the child when you talk.

  The best conversations we have come in situations where our stomachs are pointing in the same direction, in a car for example. This is because our muscle tension is best reflected when we stand opposite each other. Standing slightly turned away reduces the reflection and makes it easier for the child to retain self-control.

- Distract instead of confronting.

    By shifting the child's focus, you do away with the affect contagion that arises between you and the child in a situation where you are setting a boundary. This could mean, for example, that instead of saying, 'Stop crying', you start acting silly in order to get the child to think about something else. In the escalation phase (see Figure 6.1), distraction is probably the most important active method there is.

- Don't take hold of children with tensed muscles.

    Muscle tension is contagious just as affects are. If you have to take hold of the child, then do so calmly and follow along with his movements. Physically restraining a child by holding him tight will, in most cases, lead to violent conflict.

- Practise feeling calm.

    All the points above will automatically make you feel calmer yourself. But if you remain angry and upset, then none of the points will work completely. So it is important that you practise calming down when you end up in a stressful situation.

- Go away if you realise that you are too upset to handle the situation.

    This is one of the most important things to remember. As adults, we have to take responsibility for both the child's and our own affect levels in a conflict situation.

AFFECT REGULATION FOR ADULTS

Most parents have probably, at some time or other, pretended to be calm when they were actually angry, upset or sad, and been 'seen through' by their children. Since feelings are infectious, it's a good thing if we as parents don't just pretend to be calm, but actually feel calm. But this can be easier said than done.

In Chapter 2, 'Children Behave Well If They Can', we talked about how children differ in their ability to calm down and stay calm, an ability which is called affect regulation. This is obviously true for adults too. In the present example, Freya's father, Thomas, says to Brenda that things usually go well with Freya if you simply stay calm. Brenda probably doesn't think staying calm is 'simple'.

The good news is that affect regulation is something that keeps on developing throughout life, and it can be practised. There are also several good strategies we can use in agitated situations, strategies that are not about hiding away our feelings or ignoring them, but about actually changing them.

We have already mentioned several important strategies in the list above. Things like using a calm and relaxed posture and avoiding eye contact don't only help the child to retain control, but also make the parent calmer.

Other strategies that could be useful in an agitated situation
Expecting things to go well
When a child often acts out, as parents you can easily start expecting to get upset. It is more effective to think that things will most likely work out just fine. You have no doubt managed to stay calm many times in your life, presumably more times than your child. You will no doubt handle this

situation too. Not expecting ourselves to lose control over our feelings helps us maintain control.

Thinking about something else

It doesn't have to be something calming or positive: it could just as well be trying to remember the words of a song, counting how many round things you can see, or trying to remember what a certain person looks like. Among the most effective things to do, according to research, is to think about things that require you to use your working memory a little extra. Counting to 10 is a common recommendation which uses just this technique. But it is probably even more effective to count backwards, from 10 to 1, or to think of 20 kinds of fruit beginning with the letter A. Another common recommendation is to think of something calming, such as a peaceful place, kittens or a quiet lake. But trying to think calming thoughts actually makes some people more upset. In that case, neutral thoughts are actually better.

Movement

To move – perhaps dance, jump, move your toes or chew gum – is calming. Just make sure that your movements don't further upset the child. In the escalation phase, the chaos phase or the de-escalation phase, many children have more difficulty than usual interpreting and relating to unexpected, fast or extensive movements.

Focusing on your body

Breathing deeply or relaxing various muscles is calming, just as we mentioned earlier. But also taking note of how one's body feels has a calming effect. Listen to your own breathing. Feel your heartbeat. Think about your feet. Listening to

79

recordings of heartbeats, calm breathing, waves and other rhythmic sounds also has a calming effect. This is because it actually means thinking about something else, and because body awareness itself is calming.

Taking note of how you're feeling

Becoming aware of your feelings – regardless of whether you are trying to do something about them – initiates processes in the brain that are intended to keep us calm. This is not really surprising. Someone who has become very angry probably can't fully remember discovering that he was getting angry.

Reinterpreting the situation

Was the child trying to hit you – or was he trying to retain his self-control by making you keep your distance? Did the child not want to brush his teeth – or was he very tired? Did the teenager think that you were stupid – or did he feel run over? How we interpret a situation and what we think about what's happening affects our feelings. Just by reading this book, you have been given some ideas that will affect how you will interpret the next agitated situation. This is probably one of the reasons that Greene's statement that 'Children behave well if they can' is effective in preventing conflict.

Changing the situation's direction

This is what large portions of this book are all about, so we are sure that you as a reader already have a good idea of what this means. Take a step back. Change the subject. Take out some chewing gum. Distract with a song or a joke. Sometimes we need to let go of the demand temporarily, in order to eventually help the child accomplish what he needs to do and to remain calm ourselves.

Going away
Say 'I need a break', 'I want to think for a while' or maybe 'I'll be back in 15 minutes.' Fifteen minutes is usually plenty of time to calm down, if only you are left in peace and quiet.

Letting someone else take over, if possible
If there are other adults nearby, it can often be effective to hand over the situation to someone else who is calm, and then go away – preferably before becoming too upset.

Effective ways of improving affect regulation
In addition to strategies for calming down in the moment, there are some things that seem to be more effective than others at improving affect regulation, as described below.

Identifying what usually makes you upset
A particular child perhaps always seems to succeed in doing just the thing you hate the most, maybe spitting or using bad language. The time of day, how hungry you are and how stressed you are affect how easy it is for you to stay calm. By learning to recognise our weak points, we gain a better understanding of what we should avoid and when we need to be especially alert in order to avoid conflict.

Deciding who does what
In some families, one parent may get the children into their pyjamas without a problem, while the other always seems to end up in a fight, no matter how hard they try. In other families, the teenager invariably starts slamming doors when the conversation is about personal hygiene, but listening to what Grandpa says is no problem. Some situations are difficult to avoid, and in a family we are often the only adult around. In that case, of course, it is important to find ways

to manage them. But avoiding those particular things that have gone haywire so many times before can actually be wise planning. It is one way to be strategic as a parent – a way of choosing one's battles.

Meditation/mindfulness

Various types of training in meditation and mindfulness are available. People who use meditation in their everyday life are often better at staying calm in situations of turmoil. Exactly what happens in the brain is not known, but it appears that something about the meditation itself trains the ability to regulate affect. There are several scientific studies that have shown good results from mindfulness training for parents who have children who act out, both on the parents' stress and well-being and on the children's behaviour.

Exercise and physical activity

Being a little more active in everyday life has been shown to have a positive effect on the ability to stay calm. The same applies, of course, to well-being in general, eating regularly, sleeping and the like. But physical activity both is calming when you are upset and also appears to improve affect regulation.

Writing down what happened, preferably in detail

Studies have shown that to tell someone or write about difficult situations you have experienced has a positive effect on affect regulation. The most calming thing of all is to describe the experience itself in detail and to be as concrete as possible. Don't think so much about how it felt, why things went wrong, who was to blame or how badly it will go in future. That is not so important, either in order to succeed in the future or to calm down here and now.

Focus instead on the concrete details, such as what you saw, what you heard and what you yourself did. Simply describe what happened. It helps you feel calmer when you think back on the situation. And perhaps you will also discover things you hadn't thought of before.

PARENTS ARE DIFFERENT TOO

Brenda and Thomas in the story at the beginning of this chapter are different. Brenda gets angry more often. Thomas finds it easier to stay calm. This doesn't mean that Thomas is a better parent than Brenda. It means that Brenda has to be more aware of her own behaviour when she is with Freya.

We have written a lot in this book about how badly things can go. But we also want to write a little about how *well* they can go. Thomas finds it easy to stay calm even when Freya gets upset. Things easily turn out well. But strangely enough, as parents we rarely think about the things that go well. We think that's how it should be. We think that's normal.

If we are honest with ourselves, we have to admit that a little conflict here and there is actually what is normal in a family with children. That doesn't mean that we shouldn't bother trying to reduce conflict, but rather that it's not the end of the world if there is a bit of conflict now and then. It also means that Brenda can be an excellent parent even if she does fight with Freya occasionally. The parts that are good about their relationship are, luckily, much greater than those that aren't quite perfect.

It's a bigger challenge for Brenda to stay calm than for Thomas. But Freya loves both of her parents and needs them both. Brenda's temperament means that the relationship between Freya and Brenda is a little tighter than that between Freya and Thomas. The exchange of good feelings, like joy and love, is greater between them. Besides, Brenda knows from her own experience how difficult it is when one's feelings get the better of one. Perhaps over the years she has found strategies of her own which might also work for Freya.

We must not mistake occasional failure for lack of suitability. Brenda has an advantage when it comes to love but has to work harder to stay calm. Thomas has an advantage with regard to staying calm but has to work harder at closeness – because parents are different too.

Summary

We are all affected by each other's feelings. If we are together with happy people, we become happy. Children who act out are often more affected than others by the feelings of those around them. It is therefore important that parents not be confrontational and angry in the way they express themselves. A calm tone of voice and calm body language reduces conflict.

9

Conflicts Consist of Solutions and Failures Require a Plan

FREDDIE

Freddie is asleep. It's seven o'clock and time to get up. His father, Stephen, comes into Freddie's room, turns on the light and says: 'Time to get up!' Freddie sees it as a problem that Stephen wakes him up. He solves this problem by pulling the blanket over his head. But this Stephen sees as a problem. He solves it by pulling away the blanket. Then Freddie gets up, turns off the light and goes back to bed. Stephen takes hold of him and says: 'Ohhh no – up you get! Otherwise, you won't be in time for school.'

Freddie still sees this as a problem. 'I'm tired. Let me sleep', he says as he pulls away from Stephen's grip. Stephen starts to get irritated. He says: 'Get up! Otherwise, I'll fetch some water and pour it over you. Get moving now. I want to see you up before I go.' Stephen takes hold of Freddie's arm again and pulls at him. Freddie twists and shouts: 'Stupid idiot! Let go of me!'

Stephen lets go and fetches a glass of cold water, which he pours on Freddie: 'There. Now you're awake. Shall I get some more?' Freddie sits up, takes a swipe at Stephen and says: 'You're completely crazy!' Then Stephen grabs hold of him, drags him to the bathroom and holds the door open, saying: 'There. Now brush your teeth! Then breakfast.' Freddie shouts 'Bloody idiot!' one more time and smashes the mirror hanging above the sink.

After a while, Stephen lets go of the door and creeps stealthily down to the kitchen. When Freddie comes down to breakfast 10 minutes later, he is still angry: 'I hate you! I'm never talking to you again'. Stephen laughs and says: 'But it worked. You're up now. And the cost of the mirror will come out of your pocket money.'

HOW CONFLICTS CONSIST OF SOLUTIONS

The principle 'Conflicts consist of solutions' is clear in the example above. If we look at Freddie's and Stephen's actions step by step, we can see that the situation develops according to a simple pattern. Freddie encounters a problem. He solves it in a way that becomes a problem for Stephen, and so it goes on. The situation develops through a pattern of solutions which continually lead to problems for the other party. As the solutions progress, the level of violence increases until physical conflict is a fact.

This type of conflict can only be solved by one party finding a solution that is not a problem for the other. And here comes the interesting part. Many parents ask themselves: 'How can we get our children to find solutions that are not a problem for us?'

This is interesting because we as parents have the best potential to find an alternative solution in a situation, especially when dealing with a child who frequently ends up in conflict. We are the ones who are responsible for everyday life and for our children's well-being and development. How on earth, then, can anyone come up with the idea that problems should be solved by children? It is much easier for the parents to find a solution that doesn't become a problem for the children. In Stephen's case it's about finding a way to wake Freddie that Freddie doesn't see as a problem. Maybe do it a little more quietly. Maybe Freddie needs to be woken a few times – just as Stephen presses the snooze button several times each morning.

When parents think they have to win

In the situation above Stephen thinks he has to win. He also thinks that he can power his way through the event. In his opinion, Freddie has to change his behaviour. But this mindset deprives Stephen of the possibility to influence Freddie in the long-term perspective. The objective is presumably that Freddie will be able to get up on his own each morning. But the way it is now, Stephen's method is not helping Freddie to achieve this. Freddie thinks that Stephen is an idiot. That does nothing good for his chances of succeeding next time. The risk of failure is extremely high when we use methods such as those Stephen used. So we need to find solutions with a lower risk of failure.

A good solution must build on us not creating problems for our children. Freddie's solutions didn't have to be a problem for Stephen. He could have backed off and come back again a little later. The problem is that Stephen thinks he has to win. And that's when things get out of control, because Freddie has no intention of losing. In reality, both have lost as soon as someone considers himself the winner. Stephen will have difficulty being the person he needs to be for Freddie in everyday life after a conflict such as this.

WHY FAILURES REQUIRE A PLAN

When a method we are using doesn't work, it's usually a good idea to do things differently. It is then wise to evaluate what we have done in order to figure out what we could have done differently.

If we look back at the outburst-of-affect model (see Figure 6.1) and apply it to Freddie and Stephen's conflict, it's easy to find the affect trigger. Stephen is simply not very nice when he wants to get Freddie out of bed. It is also very obvious that the methods Stephen uses in the escalation phase don't have the desired effect; Freddie does not manage to regain control over himself. We can also see that the methods Stephen uses in the chaos phase, when Freddie is no longer in control of himself, are not very good, and that they don't lead to an improvement in either the situation or their relationship.

AVOIDING PHYSICAL RESTRAINT

Right in the chaos phase, it is important not to limit a child's freedom of movement. If we carry away or hold the child, then the chaos phase will be considerably prolonged. In addition, we have already mentioned how holding children with tensed muscles increases their own muscle tension and thereby also the stress, adrenaline rush and risk of violence. If there are siblings or other children nearby when a conflict is developing, it is usually most effective to ensure that the other children go somewhere else, rather than trying to move the child who is upset.

Physical restraint is dangerous, both for the children themselves and for the others involved. In most countries one may take hold of a child in an emergency to avoid immediate serious danger to life or health. But the fact that it is legal doesn't make it a good solution. Every time we restrain a child we increase both the risk of more frequent and more violent situations.

Using emergency measures is, by definition, something one does in an emergency. An emergency means a rare and unpredictable event. Sometimes we meet parents who tell us that they restrain their children regularly when they are violent or acting out. This can never be considered an emergency measure. If a child is violent regularly, then these are no longer unpredictable situations. Then we must instead identify what demands or expectations we are placing on the child in the situations where it happens so that we can prevent them.

It also happens that parents think they have to restrain their children because they have thrown a chair or something similar. This is totally up the wall. Often the child has already stopped throwing things when we take hold of him. Then there is no longer any danger to life or health, and so no need for emergency measures. It will just escalate the conflict and in no way prevent a similar situation from arising again.

It is also extremely frightening for the child who is being restrained. Children who are restrained are not your average children, but rather children who find it a little harder than others to manage their daily life. They are often children who have trouble judging the consequences of their actions, difficulty figuring out other people's motives and problems in regulating their affect. In other words, they are children who have immense difficulty navigating in just the kind of situation where they are restrained. When we talk to children who have been restrained, they say, for example:

- 'They held me. I don't know why. Then they shouted at me to calm down. How can you be calm when they shout like that? So I bit him.'

- 'They held me down. I thought I was going to die. I couldn't breathe.'

- 'They sat on me so that I couldn't move. It made me panic.'

- 'When someone grabs my arm, I panic. I think about when they held me when I was smaller. All the feelings I had then come back again.'

There is no research to show that restraint helps. It rather reinforces children's behaviour problems over time. Their confidence in their parents also falls; sometimes the conflicts develop into all-out war. And most important of all: Children are hurt and some even die while being restrained. In addition, restraint is about the parents being in control, not about creating self-control in the children. If we are to teach children self-control, then we can't restrain them.

As parents, then, we must avoid restraint. In the second part of the book we will look a little closer at practical things we can do instead, using different and better methods. But we also have to learn to modify situations so that they don't occur again. Every failure requires that we create a plan.

Summary
Most conflicts consist of an exchange of solutions, where each person in turn tries to solve the problem that the other person's solutions are creating for him. This type of conflict requires that one of the parties find a solution that does not represent a problem for the other party. As parents, we often try to find ways to get children to find solutions to our problems. What we should do instead is solve our problems in such a way that doesn't create new problems for the children. Then we will be spared from conflict.

10

We Make Demands of Children That They Don't Make of Themselves — But in a Way That Works

NIAMH

Niamh is 2 years old. She doesn't like brushing her teeth. Niamh's grandmother is visiting, which Niamh thinks is just great. When it's time for Niamh to go to bed, Aidan, her father, says: 'Come Niamh. Let's go and brush your teeth.' 'No,' says Niamh and carries on fooling around with her grandma. 'I'm gonna get you!' says Grandma. Niamh laughs in delight and runs away. Grandma chases her, sweeps her up and carries her off to the bathroom while saying: 'Now I've got you, now I've got you!' Niamh laughs.

In the bathroom Aidan takes out the toothbrush and toothpaste. He says: 'Come on Niamh, open your mouth. We're going to brush your teeth now.' Niamh clenches her teeth together so that he can't get at them. Then Grandma takes hold of Niamh's legs and holds her upside down. She and Niamh laugh together. Aidan takes the opportunity to start brushing while Niamh is laughing. Niamh thinks that's OK.

TAKING AWAY A CHILD'S AUTONOMY

Most of the demands that parents make in daily life have to do with getting our children to do things that they would not have done if we hadn't asked them to do them, such as getting out of bed, showering or brushing their teeth; or calming down, chewing their food or not calling people names.

The philosopher Martha Nussbaum says that what we are doing as parents is, to some degree, taking away the child's basic right to autonomy. This is an interesting and somewhat controversial way to look at the subject. But we can certainly understand how she's thinking. We actually don't allow children to decide completely for themselves what they want to do and what is going to happen during the course of the day – because they *can't* decide. The thing that characterises them as children is that they cannot make relevant demands of themselves.

That's why we adults prefer to decide the programme for the day. We set up the rules that are to be followed and we require certain behaviours of children – all for the children's own good. But this also means that we are taking on quite a large responsibility. We cannot completely take away the child's autonomy. It is, after all, a basic human right to be able to decide over you own life. Nussbaum is of the opinion that, since everyone actually has the right to autonomy, we must have good reasons when we want to limit a child's autonomy. Really good reasons. Every time.

Relevant reasons for limiting a child's autonomy
Avoiding danger
A good example is the seat belt in a car. The basic principle that applies in most of the world is that you are not allowed to lock people in or lock them in place. For this reason we

have to be able to release ourselves when belted into a car. But children in car seats can't do so. If they could, they would do it all the time. We can understand that things are arranged this way, because it protects the child from harm. This is also the argument that applies when resorting to emergency measures, for example holding onto a child to prevent him from running out into traffic.

Care

As parents, we use the care argument, for example, when it comes to our children's hygiene. To avoid danger, we can use quite far-reaching methods that border on being instruments of power and compulsion. This is not possible with the care argument. Taking hold of a child who is on his way out into traffic is not seen as abusive, but to brush a child's teeth by force is definitely going over the limit in many people's opinion. It means that the child feels vulnerable and exposed to the very people on whom he depends. When we make use of the care argument, we must turn instead to pedagogical tactics and even some purely manipulative tools, as in the situation with Niamh above. We can persuade, structure and motivate, as long as the child then agrees. But we must never forget that, even when we make decisions for the child's own good, we are limiting their autonomy. Constant ethical reflection is needed about what decisions we want to make, why and how we do it. It's not a problem when we are talking about brushing teeth, but it can definitely be one when we want to decide who our children can play with or what clothes they can wear.

Increasing actual autonomy

This is the ultimate argument. Children can't handle full autonomy. Adults probably can't handle it either. This has been grasped by society and so politicians have limited our autonomy in certain areas. A good example is traffic. Parliament has decided that we are only allowed to drive on one side of the road. This is an enormous limitation of ordinary people's autonomy, but at the same time it means that our possibilities of driving wherever we want are greatly increased. If we were allowed to choose for ourselves which side of the road we wanted to drive on, we wouldn't be able to get very far. The decision that children must go to school is built on this argument. By deciding that all children must go to school, we increase their possibilities of choosing a career. At home, we use the autonomy argument when we limit the activities from which our children can choose if they themselves are unable to get an overview of what is actually possible. They can't choose to go to a funfair on a Wednesday in November or to wear their best dress on an outing in the woods. Instead, we can offer possible alternatives: swinging in the backyard or colouring indoors, wearing the green trousers or the red ones. This argument also is weaker than the one about avoiding danger, so it doesn't give us the right to force children to do anything. But persuasion while creating structure is allowed.

Increasing actual autonomy is central to being a parent. Many children don't have the ability to structure and make good decisions about their activities. They may play the same game the whole time, because they can't think of, or can't choose, a different one on their own. This is not true autonomy. Some of them may need help from us to structure their activities and when to do them, through agreements or suggestions. With different options to choose from, they are able to decide for themselves. By limiting children's options, then, we can sometimes actually increase their real autonomy.

GETTING A YES

The other principle in the title of this chapter is also important to discuss here: 'Make demands in such a way that they work.' This is about getting the child to say yes to the demands that we are making.

Unfortunately, you don't get fitter by buying running shoes, and it may not be enough to schedule 'running' in your calendar or to get a running app. If you want to get fitter, you actually have to run. Children don't get clean teeth because we have a rule about brushing teeth morning and evening, nor if they clench their teeth when we come with the toothbrush. Making demands that are not fulfilled is pointless. For a demand to meet its objective, we have to get a yes from children. Without it, we don't achieve anything.

Sometimes parents say: 'I demand that she get up. Even if she stays in bed for several hours, I'll keep nagging at her. She's not to laze in bed all day.' This is quite absurd. If our children don't get out of bed when we demand it, then we probably made the demand in the wrong way. In that case we need to try to figure out how to make the demand in a way that works instead.

OFFER STRUCTURES THAT MAKE SENSE

One of the principles we have already looked at is 'Children always do what makes sense'. This means that, if we want to steer our children's behaviour in a certain direction (because we have a good reason to do so), we can make the right behaviour make sense.

There are different ways of doing this. The simplest way is to offer structures that make sense and support the behaviour we want. With the help of good rules that make sense, and with physical and time-related frameworks that guide children to behave well, we can create a predictable everyday life for children – and then we will have come a long way. With structures that make sense we get children to say yes to perhaps 95% of all the demands we make.

But some activities appear incomprehensible to our children no matter what we do. If these are important activities that they need to participate in, then we need to find ways to make them make sense – every time. This can be done in various ways.

How you can make activities make sense
Increasing children's sense of involvement
If children feel that they take part in selecting an activity, then it is easier to get them to cooperate. This doesn't mean that they need to decide on activities or to plan the day on the high, overall level. Sometimes involvement in the little things is enough, for example by saying: 'We're going shopping. Which coat do you want to wear?' Then we increase the child's sense of involvement at the same time as they get practice in autonomy.

Creating a sense of belonging
If our children feel noticed by us, it increases their confidence and trust. Trust is often enough to make children follow instructions and live up to demands. But we must ensure that the demands we make are not too high; if they are, trust falters and conflicts increase. We can also try to create a feeling of belonging and involvement by doing things together. If we say, 'Let's make the bed together', then it's easier to get children to participate than if we demand that they do it by themselves.

Preparing children

The better prepared children are, the fewer conflicts there usually are. For this reason it can be a good idea to use daily and weekly time plans so that they know what is going to happen. You can also announce when there are 5 minutes remaining until an activity starts or ends. This doesn't work well, however, if trying to prepare the child to stop in the middle of an activity that really has a natural end later. This often becomes incomprehensible. We can't prepare a child to leave the cinema in the middle of a film by saying, 'We'll be leaving in 10 minutes' – because, in that context, time turns into a blunt tool that can even increase the level of conflict. In the same way, we can't say to a 12-year-old: 'In 10 minutes I'll be turning off the computer'. Then it's better to let him finish the game and sit with him while he finishes so that he really does stop playing.

Outright tricks

An example of this might be prompting. If we want a smaller child to get ready to go out for a walk, it helps to hold out his coat. It's simply difficult for him not to put on his coat if we hold it out for him. In the same way, it usually works to give a teenager a towel if we want him to take a shower.

'Done'

'Done' is another trick. When one thing is just finished, it's easy to start doing something else. Some activities have a clear 'done', like eating, watching a film or playing a level in a computer game. We can use this to prepare children for a new activity. If we say, 'When you're finished watching the film we will...' or 'Come, let's read a story. When we've done that we'll...' then most children will be able to stop what they are doing and go on to something else. If you're on an outing and want everyone to be ready to go back home at the same time, you can offer an ice cream or a banana. All children stop what they are doing in order to eat. And everyone is ready to leave when the ice cream or banana has been eaten (done).

Moving the child's focus

Another trick is to move the child's focus to the thing you are going to do – to simply catch their interest – so that they feel they are on their way towards an activity rather than away from the one they were doing. This is something we often do without thinking about it when dealing with small children. We might say: 'Now we're going to the kitchen to have some chocolate milk. Who's going to stir the powder into your cup?'

Adding motivational features

It could be putting on some music when the children are going to clean up, setting up a competition when they have to do something boring, or adding fun to situations where we know there could be chaos. You make the thing the child is going to do more exciting by adding something interesting or fun.

Giving good reasons

Even small children can sometimes understand why they should do things – though not always, and rarely in a situation that is already agitated. But if we start by telling them why they should put on their snowsuit, then it might work. Here again, it is important to be careful not to have expectations that are too high. Little children don't understand why they should go to school or brush their teeth. It's too abstract and far away for them. But putting on your snowsuit because it's cold outside is closer to hand and might work; or simply opening the front door and asking the child which coat is best when the weather is this cold. A word of warning is in order here, though: When a conflict has already arisen, children are rarely capable of listening to reason – especially not if the arguments require lengthy explanation.

In the escalation phase, children's ability to listen and understand is often drastically reduced. In such a situation an explanation may place much too high demands on the children's abilities, even for children who are easy to reason with in the everyday phase. So do it before things go wrong.

Saying that you understand that your demand is difficult
Say calmly that you understand that your demand is difficult (but that you're making it anyway). It may sound crazy to think that this could help, but studies have shown that if we validate the child's feeling that it sucks to have to turn off the computer, brush your teeth or get out of bed in the morning, then the tendency to do what we ask increases – maybe because the child feels seen and taken seriously.

WHY DISTRACTION IS BETTER THAN SETTING LIMITS

One of the most difficult situations that you experience as a parent is setting boundaries. If a child is behaving in a way that requires us to go in and interrupt that behaviour, then the demand from us will often be very clear and corrective in nature. We are setting a limit in order to control them. There is, unfortunately, no evidence to show that setting limits leads to children changing their behaviour in the long run. At best, setting limits works as a way – but a risk-filled way – of handling a difficult situation in the moment.

A great deal of conflict begins in limit-setting situations. Distraction is therefore a better alternative. If adults think that a child is behaving in a way that is a disturbance, we often tell them to stop. But a telling-off doesn't change the child's behaviour in the long run. On the contrary, it increases the risk that the situation will develop into a conflict, since the child often doesn't understand why the demand is being made. Instead of telling them off and demanding that our children behave differently, we can start talking about something that interests them, for example catch their attention or get them to think about something else. Distraction is a very effective method for reducing conflicts.

Distraction is in fact about getting a child to think about something else. Parents do this all the time. We are convinced that you the reader does so practically every day. But, as we said before, as parents we may not notice when what we are doing is actually working. Distraction is an effective tool. And effective tools are something we should use a lot!

You can distract by talking about something the child is interested in, fooling around, pulling out some chewing gum when the children are tired and grumpy in the grocery store, or simply pointing at something interesting. Distraction isn't exactly rocket science and maybe it's so normal that it's difficult to see it as a method. But it works very well in many situations. Sometimes it doesn't need to be more complicated than that.

Summary

Part of being a parent is making demands of our children that they wouldn't have made of themselves. But if the children don't live up to the demands, then we haven't achieved anything whatsoever. We must therefore make relevant demands and formulate them in such a way that the children can live up to them.

11

It Isn't Fair to Treat Everyone the Same

LUCAS

Alex always sits in the front seat of the car. Alex's brother, Lucas, thinks this is unfair. So he asks their father, Ryan: 'Why does Alex always get to sit in front?' Ryan answers: 'Because otherwise he hits you and Louise' (their little sister). Then Lucas says: 'But I also want to sit in front sometimes.' 'Then you'll have to hit Louise too,' says Ryan, 'Do you want to do that?' Lucas doesn't want that.

'It isn't fair to treat everyone the same' is a classic principle. If it were fair to treat everyone the same, we would all wear the same size in clothing, regardless of age or body size. Everyone would pay the same amount of tax, regardless of income. This obviously doesn't work.

Children have different abilities and should be treated accordingly. Some manage a lot on their own, while others need more help than most of their peers. Refusing to help the one who needs help because others in the same situation don't need it is the opposite of justice.

This is not difficult to understand when it comes to the right to support in school, for children with special needs.

But it gets more difficult when it has to do with life at home in the family, and who gets to sit in the front seat of the car.

We parents do so want to be fair. We want our children to feel fairly treated. Perhaps we remember a time when we ourselves were unfairly treated and how bad that felt.

But now we'll let you in on a secret. It isn't possible to treat all children fairly – not in that to-the-millimetre way, where everyone gets exactly the same amount of everything. That's how it is. There's no point in even trying. Children have different needs, and if we don't meet those needs on an individual basis to the best of our ability, then things won't turn out very well.

We ourselves have never been fair to our children in that way. Both of us authors have children with special needs and children who are quite normal. Then it becomes especially clear and rather self-evident. One child may get to sit in front a lot, another gets help to clean his room, yet another gets financial help for some time after reaching adulthood, while the siblings don't get that help – just so that it will be fair. Every child should get help according to their needs.

Sometimes we meet parents who have done their utmost to be fair. After a while, they often discover that things didn't work out very well. Most children are quite good at finding their parents' weak points. If our weak point as parents is a desire for everything to be fair, then our children will challenge us on that point. They will charge us with being unfair and we will get a bad conscience and try to put things right, and fail. We will also lose authority, for which child can depend on a parent whom they can manipulate any way they like?

In the example with Lucas, the father, Ryan, has chosen to put Alex in the front seat to prevent fighting. If Alex sits in the back, there will be a lot of fighting. By adjusting the situation in this simple way, Alex is able to ride in the car without hitting his siblings. This is good for the whole family.

But then Lucas also wants to sit in front. If Ryan had already had a bad conscience or hadn't been clear about why he thought his solution was fair, then he might have started to get a bad conscience when Lucas wanted to sit in front. But Ryan understands that different needs require different solutions. Instead of having a long discussion about it, he stands up for his decision in a simple and clear way. He reminds Lucas that Alex isn't as good at keeping from fighting as Lucas is. And Lucas understands that it would be unfair to both Alex and Louise if he were allowed to sit up front. The placement in the front seat is due to the fact that he and Alex have different needs.

In the previous chapter we listed some ways of making activities make sense. One of them was to explain why something is to happen. This is what Ryan chooses to do, and when it comes to justice between siblings, a simple explanation such as this often works well. But if Lucas had been a child who was easily upset by inequality, then Ryan could have used some of the other points on the list in order to make it easier for Lucas to retain his self-control. He could have gone on to say that he understood that it felt unfair (validation), let Lucas choose which side of the back seat he wanted to sit on (autonomy in the little things) or put on some music that Lucas liked (distraction). Just like Ryan, as parents we must let our authority be self-evident if we are to retain our children's confidence when it comes to justice. We do this best not by yielding to our bad conscience, but by simply standing up for the fact that we treat our children differently – in order to make things fair.

Summary

Being fair as a parent doesn't mean treating our children the same way, but rather treating them in accordance with their different abilities, and standing up for it.

12

You Become a Leader When Someone Follows You

AHMED

Ahmed is 12 years old. During his summer holiday, what he would like to do most is play on the computer almost the whole time. One day his mother, Soheyla, thinks he should go shopping with her so that he gets out a bit. Ahmed doesn't want to do that, so Soheyla suggests that they could look in at the games store as well. Then Ahmed comes along.

That evening Soheyla discusses the situation with her husband, Mohammad. Mohammad says: 'How can you be so accommodating? He should surely be able to come along when you ask him. You shouldn't have to bribe him.'

A couple of days later, Ahmed is sitting at the computer again. Mohammad comes in and says: 'You're going out now.' 'That's not for you to decide, is it?' answers Ahmed. Mohammad goes on: 'You can't sit in here and hide. Get out into the sunshine!' Ahmed shouts: 'You can keep the hell out of where I sit, you damned pig!'

Mohammad gets angry, but he also knows that he can't force Ahmed out there and then. So he says: 'If you don't go outside now, I'm taking the computer away.'

HOW WE ACQUIRE AUTHORITY BY
UNDERSTANDING THE NATURE OF POWER

Authority is an interesting concept. We often don't succeed in either creating or maintaining authority by being authoritarian. Mohammad in the example above tries to win the conflict, but he loses it. He doesn't increase the chances that Ahmed will go out. In addition, most likely, Ahmed's confidence in him will decrease. To create and retain our authority as parents, we need to understand the nature of power.

HOBBES' GOVERNMENT

Seventeenth-century British philosopher Thomas Hobbes advocated a form of government which we today would call a dictatorship – a supreme ruler who decided over the people. But he also said that people give up their freedom to their leader in exchange for security, rights and care. If the leader then fails to fulfil the people's needs in these areas, they take back their freedom. We have seen many examples of this in recent years, not least the collapse of communist rule in Eastern Europe around 1990 and the Arab Spring a few years ago.

In principle, the same mechanism applies in families too. Our children give up some of their autonomy in exchange for security and well-being. If we don't succeed on these points, then children take back their full autonomy, either by calling things into question or by being rowdy. But children can't vote their parents out of office. In that sense, the family is a dictatorship.

Unfortunately, we don't always understand how badly things usually go for dictators. If we did, perhaps we would make more sure of meeting our children's needs and increasing their autonomy.

WHY WE HAVE TO DESERVE POWER

A family is not a democracy. Our children have not chosen us to be their parents. We therefore have to show ourselves deserving of power. Just to be clear: Nowhere in the law does it say that children have to do what their parents tell them. But parents do have to ensure their children's well-being. The responsibility for leadership, then, lies full and square on us.

This takes us back to the concept of meaningfulness and sense. People do what makes sense. We thus have to ensure that the behaviour we want from our children is the one that makes most sense in every situation. This leads us to the various methods we have discussed so far in this book. We have to give children understandable structures to relate to, with regard to physical frameworks as well as rules and activities. We have to instil confidence and a feeling of involvement in them – well-being, security and a good life.

NAME-CALLING

Our children are subject to our power in the same way that we all are subject to the power of the government. This carries with it a special responsibility on our part in order to maintain our authority and our leadership.

Name-calling is not unusual. It is usually used by people with the aim of evening out a perceived inequality. If two people have a relationship of equality and one of them suddenly gets bossy, then it is not unusual for the other to start calling the first person some less pleasant things.

He might say: 'Why should *you* be the one to decide all of a sudden? Bloody idiot!' Then the other one might say: 'Sorry, I shouldn't decide over you. We are equals.' Equality is restored. But he could also say: 'What? Bloody idiot yourself!' And equality is also restored. Two idiots. Is it OK to use insults in this situation? Perhaps. Most of us do, anyway.

THE RIGHT TO CRITICISE AUTHORITY

The relationship between Ahmed and his father is not one of equality. It is a power relationship. Ahmed's father is the one with the power. Ahmed's name-calling is a way of challenging Mohammad's power. What is interesting is what Mohammad may say in response. If Mohammad thinks that their relationship is one of equals, and he says: 'You are not to call me names. It's not OK', then he will lose authority in Ahmed's eyes. Mohammad says that they are equal. Ahmed will probably use more insults in the future. After all, it worked.

If Mohammad is aware of the power relationship, then he will instead say: 'You might think so, but it would be good if you went out anyway. It would do you good.' Then Mohammad may be able to save what authority he has left. His answer will also reduce Ahmed's future use of insults. Threatening that Ahmed will not be allowed to use the computer, on the other hand, will not increase Mohammad's authority.

Some parents have tremendous difficulty seeing authority in this way. They use arguments like: 'If my son is allowed to talk like that, then his siblings will do so too. Soon we'll be hearing who knows what from our children.' However, this has not been our experience. In reality, the great majority of children won't call their parents pigs just because a brother or sister does so, just as most of us don't call the prime minister an idiot just because someone does so in a letter to the paper. Our children want to have a good relationship with us. The few who don't succeed with this need a greater investment from us.

It is important to remember that insults from children are always aimed at our role in the situation, and not at who we are as people. So if your child calls you a bitch, you can calmly reply: 'No, I am your mother' (with a gleam in your eye if you can) – because it is only your role that is being called into question. Insults only mean that children think that we as parents have greater power than they do. And that's how it is, of course.

LEADERSHIP AND AUTHORITY

There are many more aspects of leadership and authority that we could discuss. Most of them have already been discussed in previous chapters, but a little repetition is always good.

If we want children to cooperate we should:

- ensure that what we want children to do is interesting, makes sense and is meaningful

- ensure that the physical environment at home is conducive to peace and quiet by, for example, choosing calm colours and dampening harsh sounds

- be present and make our children feel seen and secure, so that we deserve our authority.

We can create calm by investing in:

- structure and predictability, for example by creating plans or lists of what the children are to do during the day

- rules that make sense and that the children willingly follow because they understand them – or situations that make sense, where the most natural thing to do is the right thing

- being calm yourself

- not escalating conflicts by meeting harshness with harshness, but rather aiming for cooperation

- maintaining authority by taking it for granted and by not misusing it

- avoiding punishment, scolding and reprimands.

In Chapter 10 we spoke of how meaningless it is to make demands that children don't live up to. The same principle applies to leadership too. We only become leaders when our children follow us. And the other way round – when we give our children the opportunity to follow us, we automatically receive greater authority. We become leaders because they follow.

Summary
Authority is something our children hand over to us in our role as parents. We can make it easier for our children by treating them with respect, making sure they are secure, and making decisions when needed and not being provoked when our leadership is challenged; for example, if a child calls us names we just say: 'That may be, but come and eat now.'

Part 2

Cases and Action Plans

This part of the book is about how we can put into practice the principle that the one who takes responsibility can make a difference; how we can find the tools we need in our role as parents; and, just as importantly, knowing when to use them.

13

We Live in a Garage

Consider this simple metaphor: 'We live in a garage'. When a car breaks down, you usually take it to a garage. Put simply, you make a contract with the mechanic that he will do a job and you will pay for it.

The car owner expects the mechanic to fulfil his part of the contract and the mechanic expects the car owner to fulfil his part of the contract. The contract primarily defines who is responsible for what, and what the consequences will be if one of the parties doesn't live up to his responsibilities.

Society has made a similar contract with us as parents. We are the mechanics who are to ensure that our children feel well and that, in the long term, they will be able to take part in society on the same terms as everyone else. In the meantime, we work with service and repairs.

THE MECHANIC'S EXCUSES

As parents, we work with service and repairs, just like the garage. Let us do a little thought experiment. We are assigned to do a very ordinary tune-up: change the oil, check the lights and wiper blades, and make sure that the brakes work properly. Except that when we are supposed to be finished, we haven't managed to change the oil. Then as mechanics we could come up with various excuses:

- 'The car wouldn't cooperate during the oil change. It didn't manage to loosen the oil plug, the one you have to undo in order to let the old oil out. The car just held on to the plug. What can one do?'

- 'I told the car to change its oil. I think it's a matter of motivation. It can if it wants.'

- 'When I was going to tune up the car I drove it into the garage, and while I was doing so it started throwing its engine parts around. They flew all over the place. I obviously can't have things that way. It's just a nuisance here.'

- 'I couldn't get the oil plug out. It's a half-incher. At this garage we only use metric tools. We threw out all the imperial-measure tools because it says in all the books I've read about changing oil that the latest scientific findings indicate that metric tools work on the great majority of cars.'

- 'I had to loosen the oil plug with a hammer since I didn't have any tools that fit. Unfortunately, now you can't screw it back in again. But it's the car's own fault. It could have just done what it was supposed to do.'

PARENTS' EXCUSES

Unfortunately, we have all too often met parents who think like this mechanic. They don't understand that it is their responsibility to ensure that their children feel well and can manage in their everyday life. They also have excuses for not having to take responsibility themselves, for example that the children don't do what they're told or that the children of today do as they please. But children cannot manage on their own. Our job as parents is to ensure that they do manage. They need us because they can't take full responsibility themselves for their own life or make wise and long-term decisions.

There is another aspect that can be interesting to consider: it is more fun to be the mechanic who succeeds than the one who doesn't. When you go home from work with a feeling of having achieved what you intended, then you can relax and sleep well. You may be reading this book because you sometimes lie awake at night and think about how badly things went and how difficult it is to be a parent. This feeling we intend to dispel by giving you the tools and methods that you need. It should be fun to be a parent. If you are parent to a slightly special child, then it should be extra fun, like working with slightly special cars – and it can be, if only we can regain our curiosity and have the attitude that it will most likely turn out well, if we can just figure out how to do it. In order to regain our curiosity, we have to try to retain responsibility. We already discussed this in the first part of the book, but we will look at yet another aspect of it.

Sometimes chaos and a lot of fighting develop around certain children. Then it's easy to understand that one can feel beset by a sense of powerlessness. We adults perhaps start to say that the child is stubborn, unmotivated, spoiled or even mean. In some countries parents would even slap or spank the child. But that is not constructive. It's better for us to figure out what we can do to prevent the chaos and fighting from happening again. This can be illustrated by a fairly common situation: getting a parking fine.

THE PARKING ATTENDANT

If we get a parking ticket, we can choose to see it in one of two ways:

- I parked the car incorrectly.

- The parking attendant is an idiot.

For a car owner who sees it the first way, the chances are good that he will park the car differently the next day. Then he won't get any more fines for a while. That's the good way.

But if you take the second view, then the risk is high that you will park the car in the same place the following day – and maybe get a new parking ticket. Then the most amazing thing happens: the car owner sees that he was right – the parking attendant *is* an idiot! This doesn't mean that he parks his car better the next time; instead, every new parking ticket reinforces his opinion that the parking attendant is an idiot.

The same thing happens if we think that our children don't do what we want them to do, in order to be awkward or because they are unmotivated. This attitude leads us to place the responsibility for our failures on our children, instead of changing the way we ourselves behave. If the child's behaviour is then repeated, we receive confirmation that the child really is awkward or unmotivated. Then there is a risk that we will change our methods in a more negative direction – which increases the risk for conflict.

It is much more fun to look for ways to get your children to thrive and succeed in their everyday life.

14

Case Examples

We will now look more closely at some different situations that play out between children and their parents, and try to understand them on the basis of the principles described in the first part of the book. With the help of the outburst-of-affect model presented in Chapter 6, we will analyse the situations and make plans for how parents could act the next time a similar situation arises.

LIAM AND THE MORNING ROW

Liam is sitting in the living room watching morning TV. His mother, Helen, comes in. She says: 'Don't you need to go and get dressed, Liam?' 'Yes', answers Liam.

Helen goes into the kitchen and potters around for a while. After a few minutes, she discovers that Liam is still sitting in front of the TV: 'Why haven't you gotten dressed?' she asks. Liam answers: 'You didn't tell me I should get dressed.' Now Helen gets angry: 'Stop being silly. It's high time to get moving if you're going to be ready when it's time to go to school.' Liam answers: 'What is the matter? Why are you always mad at me? I haven't done anything. You didn't tell me I had to get dressed right this minute.' He throws a magazine on the floor and leaves the living room.

Helen follows him and sees him sitting down on the bed in his room. After a few minutes, she goes in and says: 'Get dressed now! Do as I say or there'll be no Friday treats tonight. Move it!' Then Liam shouts at her: 'I bloody well haven't done anything! Leave me alone!' He pushes Helen out of the room, closes the door and locks it.

Helen takes the key from a nearby door, manages to push out Liam's key, unlocks the door and opens it. Immediately Liam slams the door shut again. Then he starts throwing his things about, screaming. Helen opens the door again and says to him: 'Stop it! You're breaking your things! Now get dressed, get on your bike and move!' Liam screams at Helen: 'Get out of here, you stupid woman!' He hits her in the face, slams the door shut and carries on throwing his things about. After a while, Liam crawls in under his blanket and starts to cry. Helen sits in the kitchen, stressed about the whole situation. Finally, she drives off to work without speaking to Liam.

DEMANDS THAT DON'T WORK

It is not so difficult to understand this situation based on the principles we have considered so far. Helen assumes that Liam understands what she means when she asks him if he shouldn't be getting dressed. But unfortunately, Liam *doesn't* understand. He thinks it is a genuine question. Except Helen's question is really an order.

It is not unusual that children who are in rows more than others take things very literally. They can't read between the lines. This is often because they have difficulty understanding cause and effect in complex situations. It is also the reason why Liam doesn't understand why Helen suddenly gets angry, and asks her why she's always mad at him.

Liam answers quite truthfully that Helen has not asked him to get dressed – because she *hasn't* asked him. She hasn't made the demand in a way that works for Liam. She thinks that Liam answers the way he does because he's cheeky and wants to annoy her. This is why she reacts the way she does. She thinks that Liam is able to behave well but chooses not to do so.

If we look at the situation using the outburst-of-affect model (see Figure 14.1), then Helen's affect curve is on its way up before Liam's curve is. Her anger becomes an affect trigger for him. He doesn't understand the situation and his frustration rises. He goes into the escalation phase.

This brings the result that Helen in turn increases the level of affect in the situation by getting agitated herself and infecting Liam still further with her affect. When Liam then does what he can to handle the situation, locking himself in to calm down, she confronts him again and pushes the conflict to yet another level. And then Liam loses control. Helen forgets that he can't cooperate if he doesn't have self-control. Liam, on the other hand, does what he can to resolve the situation based on the resources available to him. But he doesn't succeed and therefore ends up in chaos. In this situation, Helen prolongs his chaos by increasing the demands. Finally, he calms down somewhat and goes to lie down, miserable and exhausted. And Helen still feels upset and powerless when she drives off to work.

TRUST IS GONE AND EVERYONE LOSES

Helen doesn't win the conflict with Liam. She tries to win, but since he locks himself in she realises that she hasn't won. So she prolongs the conflict by unlocking the door and continues to make demands. Who loses? They both do. Helen can't live up to her responsibility to get Liam to have a good day, and Liam is obviously not feeling OK. Who is to blame for that? Unfortunately, we have to say that Helen is. Even if Liam eventually calms down and is back in school after the weekend, this has been a tough situation for him. Helen's trust capital with Liam has also dropped, and she will find it harder to make demands of him for some time to come. Liam hasn't learned anything. He doesn't learn anything from failing.

SITUATIONS ARISE

Situations like this arise all the time. As parents we misunderstand. Sometimes we have too high expectations of our children's abilities. Sometimes we act impulsively and primitively instead of thinking before we act. It happens in every family. What is important is that, afterwards, we try to understand the situation and make sure that it doesn't happen again.

Part of the reason that situations like this arise over and over again is that our version, the parents' version, is considered to have the greatest value. If we look at Helen's actions, then she is just like most of us. She finds it difficult to admit that she's done anything wrong. She will probably have a tendency to defend her actions in similar situations in the future. After all, just like Liam, she has actually only tried to handle the situation. And Liam does have to go to school.

The problem is that Helen has significantly greater responsibility than Liam does. She should have found a solution that didn't become a problem for Liam. After all, she's the adult. And somewhere, deep down, she knows that. Helen is the one who lies awake at night and thinks about how badly everything went. She is the one who feels guilty – even though she thinks that she did the only thing she could do.

WHY WE SHOULD MAKE SURE THAT IT DOESN'T HAPPEN AGAIN

If, as parents, we want to get better at handling our children's emotional outbursts, then we have to find ways to talk about situations like this without feeling guilt or shame.

There are different ways to do this. The present authors think that the best thing to do, after a particularly violent conflict – perhaps involving insults, blows, the child locking himself in, or throwing things or furniture around – is to sit down and go through the situation using the outburst-of-affect model (see Figure 14.1). You can do this together with your partner or a friend, or on your own. When the conflict is over, go through what actually happened, step by step, and think about what you – not the child – could have done differently. Below are some questions you can use as a starting point.

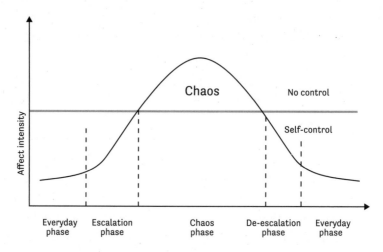

Figure 14.1 The outburst-of-affect model (from Elvén 2010)

In the everyday phase, you can ask:

1. Who said what?

2. What did I expect the child to be able to do?

3. Was the child able to do that?

4. Was there sufficient structure in the situation to help the child do what I expected him to do?

5. Was my behaviour the trigger for the child's outburst?

6. If it was, then how can I make sure that it doesn't happen again?

In the escalation phase (where the greater part of Liam and Helen's conflict took place), you can ask:

1. Which solutions did the child try to use?

2. Were his strategies actually OK?

3. Did he get the opportunity to collect himself and retain control?

4. Did I use solutions that became problems for the child, for which he then had to find solutions?

5. Did I increase the demands on the child?

6. Did I use any strategies to help the child retain his self-control (such as creating distance, avoiding eye contact, turning to the side)?

7. Did I use body language and a tone of voice that reduced the child's possibility of retaining control (a marked and insistent body language, direct and demanding eye contact, moving closer, raising my voice)?

8. Did I use any distraction strategies to actively help the child retain his self-control?

In the chaos phase, you would first ask if this was a dangerous situation, and if it was, you can ask: *Did I end it in a quick and effective way without increasing the level of conflict?*

If it was not a dangerous situation:

1. Did I manage to avoid intervening?

2. Did I use strategies intended not to increase the chaos (no eye contact, creating distance and so forth)?

In the de-escalation phase, you can ask:

1. Did the child get the necessary space and peace and quiet so that he could settle down in a good way?

2. Did I do anything that made the situation escalate again (such as scolding, reprimanding, pointing out negative consequences of the behaviour or making new demands before the child was ready for them)?

Back in the everyday phase again, you also have to ask the following questions:

1. Which structures need to be changed to make sure that this doesn't happen again, and for the situation to make more sense?

    i. Physical structures?

    ii. Rule structures?

    iii. Time-related structures?

2. Do I have a plan that I think will work if the same situation arises again?

MOVING FOCUS FROM THE PERSON TO THE METHOD

These questions are not so difficult when it comes to Liam and Helen's conflict. We can easily see that Helen didn't do much right. It is harder to be confronted with your own mistakes. If you are going to ask yourself these questions after a difficult conflict, then it is important not to think too much about what you did wrong and fret about it. The purpose of the questions, after all, is to figure out how you can avoid a similar situation in the future.

As parents we often find it easy to get a bad conscience and feel guilty about things. And that is actually a good thing.

It shows that we want our children to have a good life, that we want to do the right thing. But it is not very meaningful to get bogged down in those feelings. What is important is not who did what and why; the important thing is what we can do to prevent the situation arising again; and if it still does, what we can do then.

If the purpose is to learn to be a better parent, then it is uninteresting to talk about whose fault it was that things went badly. The methods are what is important. Preferably, the review will lead to a change in everyday structures and a plan to be followed the next time a conflict situation arises that is similar to the one just experienced.

For Liam and Helen, the changes needed are fairly simple:

- If Liam doesn't get dressed, then Helen should *ask* him to get dressed. She can even, in a nice way, offer to help him take out some clothes.

- She should not use sarcasm (sarcasm causes shame, and that increases the level of affect).

- She should make sure that Liam has a functioning structure for mornings so that he knows what to do and in what order. It's a good idea to write down the structure.

A plan for conflict resolution that Helen could use as a starting point might look something like this:

1. Stay calm.
   If Liam gets riled up, it's often because he hasn't understood. Perhaps repeat the demand in a calm way. ('Time for you to get dressed now, Liam.') If that doesn't help, move on to step 2.

2. Talk about what is going to happen.

It's a good idea to sit down beside Liam; he likes it when you chat quietly with him about how things are going. ('Wow, have you reached that level already? How are you doing on this one?'... 'Oh, by the way, you have music in school today; is anything else happening? I thought we could have pancakes later when I get home, since you're having spaghetti for lunch today.') Then start again. If this doesn't help, or if he reacts negatively to it, move on to step 3.

3. Say sorry if you've had differences of opinion.

    He reacts in a good way to that. Ask him if he's feeling stressed and would like to be alone for a while. ('Oh, sorry! I didn't realise that you didn't understand what I meant. Do you want to be alone for a little while to calm down?') If this doesn't help, move on to step 4.

4. Ask him where his schoolbag is or which clothes he is going to wear.

    This leads him on, into the things that need to be done. Keep your voice calm and friendly. If this isn't enough and he is approaching the chaos phase or already in it, move on to step 5.

5. Let him lock himself in his room; he'll open up again after about 10 minutes (and rarely does any harm in the meantime).

PLANS FOR CONFLICT SITUATIONS

A simple list, like the one above, works as an action plan for how we as parents should act when there is a conflict. The plans should preferably be individual; in other words, they should apply to a specific child or a specific situation. Five steps is just the right number. It's few enough to remember by heart but still enough to create a buffer before the chaos phase. We don't need to write action plans for the great majority of children and situations, for the simple reason that they don't get into rows that we can't handle.

A good action plan is as follows:

1. Begin by creating space for the child's own strategies for managing the situation.

    It could be running off or simply refusing. Let him do so. If this doesn't help, move on to step 2.

2. Write a list of simple distractions that have worked in the past.

    It could be going up to the child and just being there to create calm with your own calmness, repeating a demand in a quiet and reasonable way ('I understand that, but I still want...'), asking the child to carry on with the thing that you would normally do next around this time ('It's time to...', 'It's your turn to...'). If this doesn't help or if the child reacts negatively to this, move on to step 3.

3. List some active distractions that have worked in the past.

    It could be talking to the child about something he likes, joking with him or something similar. If this doesn't help, move on to step 4.

4. Write a list of powerful distractions.

    It may be allowing the child to do something he enjoys, putting aside a current demand for the moment or having the other parent calmly take over – the whole time in a calm way and with focus on the child's self-control. ('I see that you're upset. Do you want to be alone for a while?')

If this isn't enough and the child is approaching the chaos phase or already in it, move on to step 5.

5. Break off the conflict, perhaps by going away from the situation yourself or, if the child is already in the chaos phase, by waiting it out.

   Even situations where children throw furniture around come to an end. In isolated cases, for example during dangerous behaviour in connection with a violent physical fight with a sibling or other child, it may be necessary to physically separate the children. This you do by moving with the child (not holding him in one place, which increases the conflict and chaos) and then quickly moving away again. If once is not enough, do it again, perhaps several times in quick succession, until he starts to wind down. If this happens often, it is important to get training in a method with scientific basis. We recommend the Studio III method (McDonnel 2010), which is a method for handling physical aggression. There is good evidence that it can be used to handle violent situations, reduce the risk of injury and reduce the overall level of conflict in the long term. But most of the time it's enough to go away from the situation yourself. Remember that feelings are infectious! The more upset you are, the more you infect your child by remaining on the scene.

It is an excellent idea to talk to the child about what you are going to do if he gets stressed. For example, you can agree on a safe place that he can go to when things get difficult, a place where you as a parent are not allowed to come near the child. In that case, you can remind the child about the safe place as early as step 3. But it must be the child who chooses to go there, not the parent who tells him to do so.

AVA, ALICE AND THE SIBLING ROW

Ava is 13 years old, and Alice is 11 years old. They are sisters. In the afternoons after school, they are at home alone. Ava is an easily stressed girl and, when she gets upset, she often begins to cry or fight.

When the time starts getting close to five-thirty, Ava gets in a rush to go off to riding school. Her best friend, Johnny, is waiting there and she really doesn't want to be late. But she can't find her shoes. The entrance hall is narrow and lacks good storage space, and it quickly gets untidy, especially since both Ava and Alice often simply drop their things on the floor just inside the door. Just a few days earlier, their parents decided that enough was enough and that they would no longer tidy up the entrance.

Ava gets more and more upset as she searches. She throws aside sweaters and bags. Alice comes downstairs. She has been invited to the neighbour to see their puppies and is delighted. Ava looks up and sees Alice's happy expression. She interprets it as a mocking smile and gets the idea that Alice has hidden her shoes.

'What have you done with my shoes, you little brat?' she shouts. 'I haven't touched your shoes!' counters Alice, who doesn't understand what's going on. Ava picks up Alice's brand new bag and whacks it demonstratively against the stairs. 'What are you doing?' cries Alice. Ava shouts back: 'Moving your damn garbage out of the way. It's impossible to find anything here!' Alice runs down, grabs her bag and hisses: 'I haven't taken your shoes!' Then Ava grabs hold of Alice and starts to hit her. Alice fights back and scratches her in the face.

Just then their father, Peter, comes in through the front door. 'Hey, what's going on?' he calls. He goes up to the girls and takes hold of Ava so that she lets go of Alice. Alice runs up the stairs, into her room, and locks herself in. Ava runs after her. She bangs on the door and shouts, almost in tears, that she wants her shoes and that she hates Alice. Peter comes after her. He is about to take hold of her again when he sees the shoes lying tossed just inside her room. He points angrily at them and says loudly: 'Ava, your shoes are right there, in your room! Now stop making a fuss!' Ava looks up in confusion, sees the shoes and goes over to them. She sits down on the floor and starts putting them on. Peter follows her: 'You have to get a grip on yourself and stop fighting with your little sister about everything. Now go and say sorry!' he says. Ava doesn't look at him; she just stares at her shoes while tying them on. 'Do you hear what I'm saying? Say sorry to your sister *now*!' says Peter, louder than before. Ava rises suddenly, pushes her way past Peter and runs down the stairs. The front door slams shut with a loud bang. Through the wall, Peter can hear Alice crying in her room.

When the girls' mother, Eve, comes home, Peter says: 'We have to have a serious talk with Ava again. She just fights and screams, and poor Alice gets really upset!'

SOLUTIONS THAT ESCALATE A CONFLICT

This kind of situation is a daily occurrence in many families. It begins with a misunderstanding between the children and escalates because a parent takes over and increases the level of conflict. It's easy to understand that, as parents, we want to do something in such a situation. We can't just stand and watch while two children are fighting. So we try to resolve the situation. But our solutions most often lead to an escalation of the conflict instead.

The first escalation in the situation above is when Peter takes hold of Ava. It may be a necessary action in the situation.

Fortunately, he lets go again. If he had held on to her, the situation would probably have become very violent.

Then he demands that Ava say sorry. To loudly demand that a child apologise is a clear escalation, and not a particularly smart one. Do we want to teach our children to apologise even if they feel no remorse? Is that a characteristic that we want them to have as adults?

In addition, for Peter to demand an apology is a solution that contains a built-in expectation that Ava will learn something from the situation, that she will understand that she should act differently the next time. But Ava doesn't learn from failure. She's not there yet. Pointing out that she did something wrong will probably not have any effect at all.

Here we have an important key to many situations that go wrong when we deal with children who are fighting. As parents we often think that what we do in a conflict situation should both resolve the ongoing situation and also create a long-term change, so that the situation is not repeated. This usually doesn't work. Two different problems require two different solutions.

In our example, Peter should first resolve the situation going on here and now. Then he can take care of Alice, who is upset. Only after this has been sorted out can he begin to think about what should be changed so that the situation doesn't arise again.

This means that our main strategy on conflicts and acting out could be:

1. Manage the situation without escalating the situation.

2. Evaluate. What went wrong?

3. Change what needs to be changed in order to avoid repeating the situation next time.

On this particular occasion, Peter was really lucky. Ava found a good solution for taking herself away from the conflict without it escalating still further. She simply went away. The conflict could definitely have gotten even worse if she had continued to fight with Peter. But even though it worked out OK, Peter still feels powerless afterwards.

WHAT CHANGES ARE NEEDED IN EVERYDAY LIFE?

Whenever we speak to parents about situations like this, their focus is always on the chaos phase. We think, however, that there is something not quite right if this type of conflict arises at all. We therefore want to focus on the changes that need to be made in everyday life in order to prevent such situations. Ava and Alice's parents, for example, need to think about the following:

- Was your parental support good enough in the situation? Does Ava need more support when she is getting ready to go out?

- It is possible to improve the physical setup in the entrance hall? A different type of shoe stand? Clothes hooks with name tags?

- Is the strategy of not tidying up the entrance actually working?

- Does Ava eat something in the afternoons to keep her blood sugar up?

AVOIDING VIOLENT SITUATIONS

To start by focusing on what you can change yourself often works very well. But in our experience, parents have a tremendous resistance to starting at that end. Instead, they want to know how they should have handled a situation after it has already happened. The problem is that it is not enough to have strategies for handling chaos. Two children who are fighting is still a dangerous situation which should preferably be avoided.

It should not be necessary for situations to occur that are so violent that we have to intervene physically. And if they do occur, then it is absolutely essential that we be equipped with better methods than holding one of the children. That is just too dangerous. But with the help of some simple techniques, we can intervene physically without holding them immobile.

Simple rules for physical intervention are as follows:

- Separate the children by keeping them in motion.

    This is done by going in between the children, taking hold of one child's arm and moving along with his movements. If two children are going at each other, two adults may be needed, but most often it is enough to break off the one child.

- Don't use force.

    Don't use force, but movement, for example by reinforcing the child's own movements that are not directed against the other child. If you hold on forcefully, then the chaos will increase. If you move with the child's arm movements, on the other hand, then you can steer him quite easily.

- Go where the child wants to go.

    Don't resist. Movement is more important than direction.

- Release your hold as soon as possible, within a few seconds, just like Peter did.

  If the situation continues, do the same thing again. Hold on many short times rather than one longer time. If you hold on for a long time, the child will easily start to panic.

The goal, then, is to divert the child physically, not to inhibit his freedom of movement. Holding a child immobile is incredibly dangerous for the child as well as an unpleasant situation for us, and can sometimes lead to physical injury. It also costs in confidence capital.

These days, special schools, children's services and paediatric psychiatry intensive-care wards exist which don't use any restraint or other physical intervention whatsoever. They are considered unnecessary and dangerous. If it is possible to avoid them in that type of setting, then it is definitely also possible in a family setting. We simply must not hold our children.

HELPING CHILDREN SETTLE DOWN

Helping children settle down in a good way may mean creating the possibility for them to withdraw and be alone for a while, if that's what they want, or offering them a group activity that they enjoy. We don't have to worry that they might think: *If I hit my sister, then I get to play with Mum*, and therefore fight all the more. There are far too many negative experiences bound up with the fight itself for the child to make that connection. Children don't really want to fight; they want to behave well. But sometimes fighting is the most logical thing to do.

PREVENTING CONFLICT IS THE MOST IMPORTANT THING

The most effective thing we as parents can do to prevent rows and conflicts, then, is to identify what preventive measures we can use. This applies both to everyday life and to situations where things are starting to heat up. Were we close enough to the children and paying enough attention? Could we have defused the situation if we had been a little closer? Which distraction techniques would have been effective? Was there anything in the everyday structures that could have prevented the fight? Does anything need to be clarified, and should we make a new rule?

If we return to the situation with Ava and Alice and look at it in light of the outburst-of-affect model (see Figure 14.1), then we see right away that it is primarily in the everyday phase that changes can be made.

Changes that could be made in everyday life include the following:

- Build an easily accessible shoe stand where each child has their own section. Mark the section with their name.

- Tape a line on the floor a short distance into the hallway and make a rule that you aren't allowed to cross the line with your shoes on. This usually works. Visual reminders built into the environment are often very effective.

- Send a text message to Ava 15 minutes before she needs to leave, so that she has time to get ready without stressing. There are computerised calendars and mobiles that can send text messages automatically.

- Try to arrange for an adult to come home a little earlier on days when Ava has something special to do.

- Make sure that Ava really eats something in the afternoon.

Writing an individual plan for Ava in this particular situation is not relevant. Her behaviour is fully understandable. It was the way the parents acted that made the situation take the course it did. On the other hand, it could be a good idea to write a general plan with five steps that the parents can use, when arguing and fighting break out between the sisters. A plan for defusing conflicts between the children could look something like this:

1. When it seems that a conflict is bubbling up, make sure that one parent moves closer but still keeps a distance of a few metres.

   Most often it is enough for a parent to be nearby for the situation to calm down. If this doesn't help, go on to step 2.

2. Ask the children to calm down.

   Speak with a calm voice, not angrily. If this doesn't help, go on to step 3.

3. Create a distraction and give active suggestions for what the children can do instead.

   It could be an activity that they enjoy (ball games or something like that), maybe offering a snack or offering to do something together with them. You can also reinforce the distraction by actually getting out a ball, setting out a snack on the table or doing something else that you know works. Do this in a calm and friendly manner and focus on the children's self-control. If this doesn't help, move on to step 4.

4. Break up the situation by going between the children, even if they are in the middle of a fight.

    Move away any siblings or other children who may be around, in order to reduce the affect pressure on the two who are fighting. If this isn't enough or if the children are approaching the chaos phase or already in it, go on to step 5.

5. Use physical intervention to separate the children only in extreme need.

    Remember that they must be short interventions, where the child's arms are kept moving for a maximum of 5 seconds; after that you let go. If you have to intervene physically to separate the children, it is least dangerous if there are two adults present – something that may not be possible in everyday family life, but still something to be considered. Also make sure that what you do doesn't feel domineering or abusive to the child, because this both increases the affect and reduces your authority. If you reach step 5 in a conflict, then you should evaluate what happened using the questions on pages 122–124 – because, as mentioned, this is a matter of extreme need.

SIBLING FIGHTING

The fighting between Ava and Alice is what we call sibling fighting. They probably would not have fought in the same way with a friend. A sibling has a special place in a child's life, but not always in a positive way. A sibling is someone you know better than anyone else, including his weak points.

It's someone you don't worry about losing status with. This means that children are often a lot meaner towards their siblings than towards other children. As parents, this can be difficult to take. Our picture of family life as an oasis of peace and happiness suffers a dent every time our children fight with each other.

In Chapter 2 we said that parents sometimes see it as something unnatural when their children fight. Many parents see sibling fighting as something that should not exist. But siblings have always fought. It is important and good training in social competence. They would rather train with someone they know will be there for them when they need it than expose themselves to social risks by fighting with other children.

This obviously doesn't mean that we should leave our children to handle all sibling fighting on their own. Children need support in their learning. But not in the form of us telling them what they are doing wrong. They don't learn anything from that. We may often need to help avert a conflict. If we help children find ways of not beginning to fight in a difficult situation, then they get training in avoiding conflict and making use of better strategies instead. We also need to support them in making up again, and maybe we can try to reduce the amount of fighting by having a functioning everyday structure. Children fight more with their siblings when they don't know what to do than when they are engaged in functioning, structured activities.

This means that perhaps a situation like Ava and Alice's doesn't really need to be analysed. Ava knows that it went wrong. Alice, for her part, knows that she didn't do anything wrong. But the sisters both have a feeling of having failed – something children of this age are fairly used to, as mentioned earlier in this book. Ava and Alice will most likely start afresh the following day. Ava's trust capital with Alice will probably be somewhat diminished, and she may have to be extra nice for things to run smoothly – but not for sure. What *is* for sure, though, is that neither Ava nor Alice will learn anything new if their parents don't involve them when they talk about the situation. It's much better if everyone cooperates in creating good structures. You could, for example, start by saying: 'Yesterday afternoon wasn't very nice. We've been thinking about how we can avoid this happening again. This is what we think.' Then the parents explain their ideas to Ava and Alice. Afterwards, they can ask: 'What do you think about it? Do you have any other good ideas?'

Children are more likely to follow structures that they themselves have helped to create. But there's no guarantee. If more, similar situations arise, then we have to be prepared to think further and make new changes, in a different way. It's just as well to be prepared for constant change. There are no everyday structures that always work 100%.

Constant sibling fighting

Sometimes we meet families where the siblings fight violently every day. This can be extremely trying for the whole family and sometimes for the relationship between the parents. This often happens because one or several of the siblings have problems with their skills in social intercourse, and maybe with flexibility and impulse control. As a parent, you therefore really must find an attitude that doesn't place the responsibility on the children; otherwise, the only result will be still more conflict in the form of reprimands and punishment. Family life becomes full of conflict and no one is happy. Here, too, there are some good tricks you can use:

- Children who are doing different things in different places don't fight, so avoid common activities for siblings who fight a lot with each other.

- Children who know what to do usually do so.

    Good everyday activities that have a well-thought-out structure for each one of the siblings help in most cases.

- Put siblings who fight a lot at opposite ends of the dinner table.

    Same thing in the car. This is actually pretty obvious. Get more than one TV, tablet and game console, if possible. Some children have great difficulty in sharing things with siblings with whom they often fight. Perhaps the family can't afford the most expensive one if two are needed, but rather that than constant bickering.

- Create clear structures and rules about taking turns with the things of which you can't have more than one.

    Be specific! Decide, for example, that on Mondays and Wednesdays one child gets first say about what's on TV (maybe for a specified time), and on Tuesdays and Thursdays, another. This is much easier for children to remember and handle than vague rules such as 'every other time'.

- Change the rules or routines around situations where fighting often starts.

    Maybe everyone in the family doesn't really have to eat at the same time or in the same room. Maybe the times need to be changed for doing homework, playing on the computer, watching TV, listening to music, getting up in the morning or something else. Admittedly, this may mean that as parents we sometimes have to give up our own preconceived notions of how things should be. But if we don't change the conditions, then neither can we expect the fighting to diminish.

- Remain aware that a lot of fighting starts when the children – or we adults – are hungry or tired.

  It might be before meals or when the children come home from school or we come home from work. This means that it is often possible to predict the time of day when there will be fighting, and that we can plan functioning activities, a snack or a time for rest. Remember that we adults also need to rest and eat at strategic times in order to have the strength to prevent conflict.

- Keep an eye out for situations where the children don't fight, if there are any.

  What's different then? Try to make use of this in other situations too. Do more of the activities that work. More time spent in situations that work means less time in conflict.

- Make sure to prepare for group outings with good structure.

  If the family is going to decide together, on the go, what is to happen, then there will definitely be trouble. Instead, make a plan for the day. Decide in advance where you will eat and when you will start for home. And by all means let the children be part of the deciding; the structure can be put together well in advance together with them. But it's important to remember that it's always the parents that have the final say.

- Don't see sibling fighting as parenting failure.

Rather, try to see it as a situation that partly needs to be solved here and now, and partly needs to be prevented in the long-term perspective. Then it will be easier to stay calm. We have said it before, but it bears repeating: Siblings do fight with each other. It's something very normal.

ALVIN WANTS TO BE ALONE

Alvin is a tall, gangly teenager. Almost every day when he comes home from school, he goes straight to his room and shuts the door. When inside, he sits at the computer, draws manga comics, reads or listens to music. Alvin's father, George, admittedly thinks that it's good to have interests, but today he thinks it would be nice if Alvin spent some time with the family. So, when he gets home he knocks on Alvin's door and says: 'Would you please empty the dishwasher?'

But all that happens is that Alvin turns up the music. George knocks again, opens the door slightly and repeats his request. But Alvin is tired and wants to be left alone. 'Not now, I'll come later', he says from his desk, where he is sitting drawing. 'Emptying the dishwasher doesn't take long', answers George. And you also get to spend some time with me and Sophie in the kitchen. She has a homework assignment to make a list of the interests the people in her family have. She would really like to write about manga. Come on, it'll be fun.' Alvin answers very grumpily: 'Why do I always have to do everything? Why can you never leave me alone?' George gets a bit annoyed and says: 'Now wait a minute, young man. I've worked all day and now I'm going to both fix dinner and help Sophie with her homework. The dishes don't put themselves away. Helping with that is the least you can do.'

George's irritation grows and, while talking, he takes a couple of steps into the room towards Alvin. He's done nothing but ask a perfectly reasonable question. Why does the kid always have to fight about little things? Then Alvin gets up a bit jerkily and takes an angry step forward. He's head and shoulders taller than his father. 'You can never get any peace and quiet in this damned family! Why are you always nagging at me?' he shouts.

'Actually, I wasn't nagging, I just asked you to do one simple thing!' George shouts back. 'It's really not asking a lot from you to say hi to us now and then, or to help out a little. You're the one who's grumpy and irritable and rude every day. We actually haven't done anything to deserve being treated in this way. Why do you always have to fight about little things?' 'Bloody idiot!' yells Alvin. 'Go to hell!' George answers: 'If you're going to carry on like that, you needn't come at all.' Then he stomps away towards the kitchen. Behind him the door slams and he hears the key being turned. *Ungrateful kid*, he thinks.

Alvin turns the music up a few notches more. Then he sits on the bed and stays sitting there for a long time.

CONFLICT AGAIN

George and Alvin's conflict is interesting. It's quite a common one, but George and Alvin interpret it in completely different ways. It all begins with the fact that George has a problem. He thinks that Alvin should come out of his isolation.

He tries to solve this problem by making a demand. George himself probably thinks that he is asking Alvin to come out to the kitchen and socialise with the family. But Alvin experiences George's solution as a problem. He doesn't even hear that George wants to socialise or that Sophie wants to hear about manga. All he hears is that he has to empty the dishwasher. This he sees as a problem. So he argues back, just like millions of other teenagers do all over the world. George sees it as a problem that Alvin argues back. This problem he thinks he can solve by arguing back again – and finally by getting angry.

There are many aspects to this situation. It has to do with being an individual or a part of a family. It has to do with different expectations. It has to do with being clear or unclear.

EXPECTATIONS

George has the expectation that a family should spend time together. This he has acquired by being Alvin's father for many years. When Alvin was little, he was keen for the family to spend time together, preferably all the time. Most children think this way. Children want to be with their parents and preferably have their full attention all the time.

But in their teens, most young people want to be alone instead, or with their friends. Parents become less important. Few 15-year-olds hang out in the kitchen with their parents just because the parents want them to do so. George probably hasn't noticed this, and maybe he misses having Alvin in the kitchen together with him and Sophie.

Alvin has no expectations about the family spending time together in the kitchen in the afternoons. All he expects is to be able to decide over his own time. Nor does he have an image of himself in which the most important thing is to be part of the family. That's what it was like when he was smaller, but with his teens came the perception of first and foremost being an individual.

Alvin is developing into an adult who first takes care of himself, and eventually, perhaps, his own family. He doesn't feel any responsibility for the household from which he is in the process of breaking free. This is quite normal. George and Alvin simply have very different expectations of family life.

CLARITY

One thing George could do is to be clearer. What he really wants, of course, is for he, Alvin and Sophie to spend time together in the kitchen. But since he knows that Alvin probably won't buy that demand, he makes a different one that he thinks makes sense to Alvin – to empty the dishwasher. The problem is that, on the contrary, this demand is actually incomprehensible for Alvin. In the discussion that follows, George mixes up emptying the dishwasher, having a pleasant time with the family, helping Sophie with her homework and talking about manga into a mishmash of information through which Alvin can't navigate. All that Alvin hears is that he can't decide over his own time.

On the other hand, Alvin, is not very clear about his wish to be left in peace. Maybe he is tired, just as he says. And maybe he would consider joining them in the kitchen later. But what he's saying sounds to George mostly like excuses. But – and this is important – Alvin is not a parent. It is George's responsibility to lead a conversation that works and to find out exactly what Alvin really means.

Instead, they leave the conflict with two different views of it. George thinks that Alvin doesn't want to socialise and be part of the family. Alvin thinks that George just nags about duties and housework, and doesn't respect his right to autonomy.

WHAT DOES GEORGE REALLY WANT?

If George doesn't want to end up in the same situation again, it might be a good idea for him to think about what he is really after: company or housework. Maybe it's both.

To achieve this, he can make various adjustments to the daily routine:

- Can he introduce a routine that puts Alvin in the kitchen as soon as he gets home, instead of in his bedroom (for example, by offering a snack right when Alvin gets home)?

  Sophie usually gets home earlier and always goes and sits in the kitchen straight away, so she is already there.

- Can he organise regular household chores?

  To get a teenager to help with a boring household task just when the need arises is difficult. It is much easier to decide in advance what the children are to help with, so that Alvin and Sophie know what is expected of them. Personal responsibility is good in many ways. George has to make sure that the children actually can manage to live up to the demands he makes. Maybe a time-related structure is also needed, for example that they always do their chores as soon as they get home or straight after a meal, maybe with the help of a reminder through their mobile phone. Few children and young people are able entirely on their own to interrupt an interesting and enjoyable activity in order to perform a task that they have been asked to do. And children are fully aware that it is the parents' responsibility that the household functions.

- Can he introduce a fixed time for help with homework?

  In other words, can he give a fixed time when Alvin helps Sophie with her homework? Perhaps this could be only once a week.

- Can he find a way for Alvin to get more energy?

As we have already noted, teenagers like to decide over their own time. Many are also more tired than they were when they were younger. If Alvin seems unusually tired, the most effective change George can make may have to do with giving him more energy. We have already suggested a snack each day when Alvin comes home. For Alvin to have some quiet time in his room is not a bad idea in itself. But can George also review Alvin's evening routines, bedtimes and sleeping habits? If Alvin has been more tired than usual lately, maybe there is some physical reason that George hasn't thought about, like pollen allergy or something similar.

- Can he introduce a regular family activity that both Alvin and Sophie appreciate?

  George wants himself and his children to spend more time together. But when children get older, the rules change for how they want to interact with others. Teenagers often want a more specific reason if they are to spend time with their parents, such as watching a game together, or going to exercise or eat out together; or that you simply take the opportunity to chat with your teenager when you're together anyway, while out driving.

It can also be an idea for George to think about his own role in the situation:

- Can he be clearer about what he wants when he asks Alvin for help? The goal, after all, is for them to spend time together, not all the other concrete demands that ensue.

- Can he explain that he thinks it would be nice if they could spend some time together each day – not in a situation where the demand exists, but at another point in time?

- Can he view Alvin's private time in his room as something that is good for Alvin in his development towards becoming an independent adult?

- Has Alvin actually become too old to socialize in the kitchen in the way that George wants?

Alvin is old enough for George to have a discussion with him. If George sits down and asks, Alvin will probably have lots of ideas about how they could compromise, so that they both get what they want: in George's case, more time together; in Alvin's case, more time to do what he wants. It is probably not the case that Alvin never wants to be with George and Sophie. But they have ended up in an unfortunate tug of war – one that it is George's job to avert, because it is always the parent who needs to make sure that you are pulling in the same direction and not in opposite directions.

A PLAN

There was a row. That happens every now and then when you have teenagers. It can therefore be a good idea to have a plan ready for what you will do when there is a row, so you have time to put on the brakes before it turns into a real fight. Since a row is not as serious as a fight, the following five-step plan is a little milder.

1. If Alvin starts to argue, then it's a good idea for George to repeat his demand in a calm and friendly tone of voice, and then leave.

Most of the time, Alvin will do what George has asked after a little while. If this doesn't work, George goes on to step 2.

2. Repeat the demand in a calm and friendly tone of voice.

   It's not a bad idea for George do it with a gleam in his eye: 'Did you forget (wink, wink)?' If this doesn't help or Alvin reacts negatively, then George moves on to step 3.

3. Ask calmly and in a friendly way why Alvin doesn't want to do what he's asked.

   There is probably a reason. Maybe he's doing something he wants to finish first. The fact that George asks 'why' gives Alvin a feeling of being seen and respected. This increases the chances that he will in fact do what George wants him to do. And if the reason is relevant and more important than the demand, maybe it's OK to let it go. If it's a demand that can't be neglected, then George has to explain this to Alvin. But also he has to explain that he understands that it feels difficult for Alvin. If this doesn't help, George goes on to step 4.

4. Let go of the demand.

   George must explain in a calm and friendly manner that he is letting go of his demand – though not say that he is dropping it because Alvin won't do as he's told, but rather because he understands Alvin's argument from step 3. If this doesn't get Alvin to wind down, then George goes on to step 5.

5. Leave Alvin's room.

   Alvin most often stays there and sulks. George must ignore this for the time being. When Alvin eventually gets in touch again, he may still be sulky. George should let him be, because it will pass. If George tells him off again, it will just refuel the conflict or start it over again. Nor does Alvin need to say sorry. He has the right to his feelings and neither of them have done anything wrong. Alvin never gets physically violent, so no plan is needed for stopping him physically.

HANNAH AND TOOTH-BRUSHING

Hannah's cross. She thinks her mother, Camilla, is mean. Camilla wants Hannah to go to bed, but Hannah doesn't want that. So when Camilla yet again tells Hannah to go and brush her teeth, Hannah says: 'You disgusting old cow! I don't want to go to bed yet!' Then Camilla raises her voice: 'Don't you call me a cow. Go and brush your teeth *now*!' Hannah carries on: 'Cow, cow, cow!' Camilla takes hold of Hannah's arm and pulls her out to the bathroom, takes out the toothbrush and says: 'Now! Brush your teeth!'

Hannah takes the toothbrush and throws it at the mirror. Then she turns and spits in her mother's face. Camilla grabs Hannah's arm again – hard, so that it hurts: 'Don't you spit at me. Either you brush your teeth now or I'll do it for you!' Hannah spits again, pulls loose and runs into her room and locks the door. Through the door Camilla hears her saying: 'Cow, cow, cow!'

WHAT COULD CAMILLA HAVE DONE INSTEAD?

This situation starts badly and goes from bad to worse. This is because both Hannah and Camilla are fighting. Hannah's affect infects Camilla, who reacts with anger, which in turn infects Hannah. If Camilla had had a conflict plan ready, she would have been able to handle the tooth-brushing conflict differently.

Now we will take the strategies we talked about in the first part of the book and apply them to a conflict plan that Camilla can use in similar situations.

Camilla's plan is as follows:

1. Create distance.

   Take a step back. If Camilla approaches Hannah, then her stress increases.

2. Camilla mustn't look directly at Hannah for more than a few seconds at a time.

   After that, she looks away for a while. This is normal eye contact in relaxed situations. She should stand slightly turned away from Hannah, with her side to the child. She should not stand directly facing Hannah, but rather in the way you stand when you meet someone you know on the street. She should speak with a normal voice, in a calm and friendly way.

3. She can create a distraction.

   Maybe by saying 'moo' the first time Hannah calls her a cow, while still keeping her tone of voice light.

4. She should repeat the demand for tooth-brushing calmly.

   At the same time, she can validate Hannah's feelings by saying: 'I understand that it's no fun, but I still want you to brush your teeth now.'

5. If this doesn't work, she should repeat the demand in a different way, for example by saying: 'Do you want to brush your teeth with the green or the red toothbrush?'

   If Hannah is 10 years of age or older, Camilla could can adjust this by saying: 'Do you want to brush your teeth now or after undressing?' Or give her another 10 minutes. There are many ways for Camilla to adjust the demand without letting it go. She must keep the goal in sight, not the demand.

If Camilla had acted this way, then the situation might have developed like this:

Hannah is cross. She thinks that her mother, Camilla, is mean. Camilla wants Hannah to go to bed, but Hannah doesn't want that. So when Camilla yet again tells Hannah to go and brush her teeth, Hannah yells: 'You disgusting old cow! I don't want to go to bed yet!' Camilla smiles at Hannah and says theatrically: 'Moo, moo.' Hannah carries on: 'Cow, cow, cow!' Then Camilla says: 'Are you the calf then? Come, let's go to the bathroom, I'll be the cow and you can be the calf.' Camilla starts lurching unsteadily towards the bathroom. Hannah can't keep from laughing. She says: 'Mummy! Cows don't walk like that,' but follows her into the bathroom anyway.

Camilla takes out the toothbrush, puts on toothpaste and holds it out. But Hannah carries on: 'No! Not yet.' Then Camilla takes out her own toothbrush, puts toothpaste on and says: 'Shall we brush our teeth together, you and me, or do you want to brush after I've done mine?' Hannah says: 'You first.' So Camilla brushes her teeth and then helps Hannah. Afterwards, Camilla takes out Hannah's pyjamas and says: 'Do you want to put on the trousers first or the top?'

Sometimes parents get very provoked when we use this type of example. They think: *She should do as I say*; or they say: 'If she's allowed to carry on like that, she'll never learn.' But the goal for us as parents can't be to get children like Hannah to obey; instead, we should teach them to make good decisions themselves. Camilla's method in the second situation, where she succeeds with the tooth-brushing, builds on Hannah constantly being trained to make her own, good decisions.

In the tooth-brushing situation, the intention is not for Hannah to learn anything. The goal is simply for her to brush her teeth and go to bed. That's all. No method that Camilla can use when Hannah starts snapping at her will get her to do what Camilla says the next time she has to brush her teeth, or in similar situations in the future. And she definitely won't learn anything from fighting with her mother.

On the other hand, Camilla's method in the second example, where she stays calm and manages to treat her nicely the whole time, increases the chances that the next tooth-brushing event will go well. Since it went well the last time, neither Camilla nor Hannah will expect trouble.

Camilla is clear throughout the situation. She chooses a gentle approach. This method simply works better, both for Hannah and for many other children.

15

The Principle of the Gentle Approach

ERIN

Erin is stressed. She has a maths test tomorrow and knows she won't pass. She should be sitting at the kitchen table studying maths. But she can't study. When Erin gets stressed, it's hard for her to sit still. She gets loud and annoying, wanders about and is grumpy and irritable. Her mother, Liv, knows this, and she also knows that Erin often ends up in fights.

Liv wants to get Erin to calm down. But she knows that the more she asks, the more Erin will protest. That's how it is when she is stressed. Nor can she be distracted, because she usually sees through attempts at distraction. She is certainly not going to let herself be manipulated.

Liv goes up to Erin and says: 'I know you're stressed. What I would really like to do is tell you to go to your room and watch a film, or that we could drink a cup of tea together so that you can calm down. But I know that you don't want to do anything I tell you to do just now. Do you have any ideas about how we can make you feel a little better?'

THE GENTLE APPROACH

We want to round off this book with a final little reflection about how we treat people. We have talked about how the ways in which we manage our children when they fight, either with their parents or their siblings, are affected by our conceptions both about the children and our own role. We have also described methods for making demands and handling conflict, methods which are based on the approach known as the low-arousal approach. In this final section we want to remind you as a reader of a simple truth: It doesn't have to be so complicated to solve conflict situations. Sometimes it can be the tone of voice or a gentle approach that makes all the difference.

We sometimes meet parents who think that they use a low-arousal approach towards their children. They have tried to distract ('I told him to go find a comic, but when he didn't want to do so, there was nothing I could do'); they have tried to adapt their behaviour to the situation; and they have carefully told their children to calm down. Put simply, they have tried to use low-arousal methods, but without changing the basic power relationship between themselves and their children – because beneath it all, they still think their children ought to understand that it is the parents who decide. They try to use the methods we have described in this book to control their children's behaviour in a way that their children don't want (to be controlled). But with that attitude, it's not going to work.

The low-arousal approach is about us as parents increasing our children's security, their feeling of involvement and autonomy, and not about tricking them into obeying.

We can learn from dementia care, in which there is a completely different starting point: People with dementia have decisions over their own lives. When their difficulties become great enough, they are moved into an environment where suddenly there are staff who decide for them. At the same time, they have so much trouble understanding and remembering where they are, and why, that they don't realise that they need help to make their daily life work. This means that, most of the time, they won't take orders from the staff. When the staff then need to make necessary demands of them, this is done in such a way that the elderly perceive it as if they themselves are choosing what is to be done.

If we take the same approach in a family, then everything gets so much simpler. Actually, then we are back to the concept of involvement, which we talked about in Chapter 9, and about pulling in the same direction instead of opposite directions. If Erin feels that Liv takes her seriously and meets her in her situation, then perhaps she can find a way out of her stress. Liv asks Erin if they can cooperate. And she does it by confirming (validating) Erin's perception of things. Erin is stressed. Liv validates this. She lets Erin know that it's OK to be stressed, that Liv knows that it's tough, and that she would therefore dearly like to offer her daughter a way out. This is one of many ways in which we as parents can work with the gentle approach.

LEO

Leo ought to go to bed. He knows that. It's nearly midnight and he needs his sleep in order to feel well. He's sitting at the computer in his room, just waiting for his mother, Anna, to tell him to go to sleep, although actually he doesn't think she has any right to decide when he should go to bed. He starts building up anger towards her because she thinks that she can decide for him on his bedtimes.

Anna goes past Leo's room on the way to her own bedroom. She asks him: 'My bed's causing trouble and I'm going to fix it. It squeaks every time I move in it, so I'm going to oil it. Do you want to help? And shall we have a look at yours afterwards, so that you can go to bed?'

PUTTING THE DEMAND IN THE SUBCLAUSE

This situation describes another way of working with the gentle approach, which is to use a subclause when talking to kids. An example of this is that Anna in the situation above doesn't focus on the demand that Leo must go to bed, but rather on something else, which gives him a chance to go to bed without actually submitting to her authority. The fact that she makes her demand in a subclause causes Leo's feeling of inferiority to disappear. At the same time Anna offers, through the question and fellowship in the situation where they're going to fix the bed, a feeling of involvement – all with a gentle approach.

As parents, we often want to be direct and clear. This is good. But some children have a hard time falling in line with other people's wishes. In these cases a low-arousal approach, in which we adjust our approach so that the child's affect is not increased, can be effective. This you can achieve through good planning and with the help of the methods we have discussed in this book. But it is also possible to take the gentle approach one step further.

The gentle approach doesn't mean that we as parents are softies but rather that we plan and carry out our everyday life with our kids in a way that is effective and gives them a sense of autonomy. It is a small way to increase their chances of success – a little fine detail without the goal being changed.

PARENTS WHO ARE UNCLEAR

Some of the parents we meet get incredibly provoked by the principle of the gentle approach. They think that their kids should do what they tell them to do. Psychologists call this style of parenting a controlling style. With it, you use scolding, punishments and consequences, but also rewards, all with the goal of getting the kids to do what you want them to do. This type of parent thinks that the gentle approach is to make life unrealistically easy, to spoil the child. We don't think so. As long as we as parents are clear about our intentions and what we ask of our children, then it is not wrong, and it won't have negative consequences in the long run.

What is most important in all this is that we keep our eyes on the goal – on what we want to achieve with our actions. Anna's goal is for Leo to go to bed. Liv's goal is for Erin to calm down. Neither Anna nor Liv are coddling their children; rather, they are clear about what they want the children to do, but they have a gentle way of talking to them.

On the other hand, if parents are unclear about what they want, despite their gentle approach, it can create conflict instead. Some children have a hard time working out other people's intentions and have problems in understanding when, for example, we are just chatting or when we are not saying exactly what we mean.

CONNOR

Connor is playing on the computer. He does this quite a lot. His mother, Emma, knows it's hard for him to stop playing in the middle of a level, for example when it's time to eat. She has often said, 'Time to eat', and been told that she is a bitch because Connor can't stop just like that. So she wants to try something new. When the food is ready she stands in the doorway of his room and waits. This stresses Connor immensely. So he says: 'What do you want? Don't just stand there like that.' Emma answers: 'We're going to eat. But I don't want to interrupt you in the middle of a level, so I'll wait until you're ready.'

Connor doesn't know what Emma wants. He can't figure out that when she's standing at his door and it smells of food, then it's probably because dinner is ready. His ability to work out other people's intentions is not very good. Social skills are normally distributed, just like all other personal qualities we have as humans. Some kids are very good at calculating other people's intentions, most do it pretty well, but for a few it is extremely difficult to handle a situation like the one above.

That Connor doesn't know what Emma wants is difficult for him. Emma's approach therefore becomes too gentle. It becomes unclear. In Connor's case, the smartest thing would probably have been to say, 'Dinner's ready. Come when you can' – because Connor can't handle breaking off his game in the middle of a level. But he still needs clarity.

BEN

Ben and his big brother, Matt, are playing with Lego in Matt's room. Ben is 8 years old, Matt 13 years old, and so Ben has to go to bed earlier than Matt does. Their father, Christopher, comes into the room and asks: 'Ben, can you go to the bathroom and brush your teeth now?' Ben agrees. Yes, he can. But he carries on playing. After a while, Christopher comes back: 'Ben, can you brush your teeth?' 'Absolutely', answers Ben, and he keeps on playing. After a few more minutes, Christopher comes back again. This time he explodes: 'Why do you never do what I tell you to do? When I ask you to brush your teeth, you do it. You don't ignore me like that. Now go and brush your teeth or I'll carry you to the bathroom!' Ben is at a complete loss: 'You didn't tell me to brush my teeth.' Christopher gets even angrier: 'And don't answer back! I did so tell you to brush your teeth. But you just pretend not to notice, as usual! Now do as I say!' Ben runs off to his room and slams the door, yelling: 'Damn useless Dad! You're always shouting at me!'

With a kid like Ben, who also has a hard time working out other people's intentions, things can go wrong in many ways. One is that as parents we are a little too vague, like Christopher in the story. He doesn't actually *tell* Ben to brush his teeth; he asks Ben if he can do so. And Ben answers, truthfully, that he can both go to the bathroom and brush his teeth.

Most kids would understand that the questions were really a request, but not Ben – he interprets the questions in a concrete and literal way. Our ability to read between the lines and work out other people's intentions is connected with our ability to see beyond the concrete. This means that children who have difficulty in calculating parents' intentions often take what we say very literally. And that easily leads to conflict in the interaction between parents and children.

Christopher has too high expectations of Ben's ability to read between the lines, so Christopher's outburst comes like lightning from a clear sky for Ben. He is totally taken by surprise.

Christopher is not clear enough when he asks Ben his question, but he is not aware of this. He probably thinks he has been very clear. His way of asking Ben is actually an attempt on his part to use a gentle approach. But he fails – he isn't clear enough for Ben.

PUSSYFOOTING PARENTS

Some of the parents who are so careful that they become unclear about their goals become what we call pussyfooting parents. They might be parents who find their children's emotional outbursts so difficult that they try to avoid the child getting anxious or angry. They don't dare to make demands and the result is partly that they become much too gentle in their approach, and partly that they become unclear about their goals.

Perhaps they don't make the demand clearly enough that it's time to eat, but just say: 'Food's ready. If you want food, it's here. But if you don't want to eat, that's OK.' They avoid certain topics of conversation because they are afraid that their children will get angry. They adjust their whole lives in order to avoid their children having any hardships. Instead, they pussyfoot around them, feeling slightly stressed the whole time. This is devastating.

Pussyfooting parents don't pussyfoot because they want to protect their children from feeling anxious or angry. They pussyfoot to avoid feeling anxiety themselves when their children get angry. But since affect is transmitted, their children are affected by their own anxiety. And then the children's anxiety can also grow.

If we look back at the situations with the mothers Liv and Anna, then pussyfooting is not what they are doing. They are simply carrying out a thought-out action with a clear goal. To help them they have good methods, such as working with validation, involvement and subclauses. The gentle approach therefore becomes an excellent way for them to help their children do what they need to do, at the same time as the children have a good day and feel seen and respected.

That's just what our job is as parents.

16

Summary

Now the book is nearly at an end. We hope that you feel it has been worth the effort to get to this last chapter. We have written about lots of principles and described situations from everyday life in different families. The things we have described are very important:

- Our kids are human beings and should be treated as such.

  They have rights just like everyone else. We as parents only get to borrow them for a while, but we have the responsibility to ensure that their rights are not taken from them during that time.

- Our children should be treated with respect; that way we teach them to treat others with respect.

- Our children should not learn to obey.

  They should learn how to make good decisions in their lives. As parents, we don't want them to be obedient as adults, but rather independent. We must therefore train them to be just that, not to obey.

- Our children need to learn to gain and maintain control over themselves.

  We don't teach them this by taking control over them, but by helping them to gain and maintain their self-control.

- And *most* important: It's we as parents who should solve the problems that arise along the way, not by thinking that our kids ought to behave differently, but by changing our own behaviour – because then we actually gain the possibility of affecting both our own everyday life and our children's development.

Good luck with being a parent! Sometimes it can feel rough, but it is the finest and most important thing there is.

Part 3

Extra Materials

Study Materials

We are pleased that you are interested in going into more depth in this book. In the following you will find some discussion questions about the book, principle by principle. Perhaps you can discuss them with a partner or friend, in order to exchange thoughts and experiences. The questions also work as discussion material for a parent group. Or perhaps you just want to take an occasional quarter- or half-hour yourself to delve into some part of the book that especially interests you.

PART 1: PRINCIPLES

Chapter 1: Who Has the Problem?

Much of what we perceive as fighting and problems with our children is only a problem for *us*. Many times the child sees the fighting or problem as a solution.

Discuss

- Find some examples of situations at home where something that you thought of as a problem definitely wasn't a problem for the child.

- Was it clear in some of these situations that it was the difference in how you as a parent saw the situation and how the child perceived it that led to escalation of the conflict?

Chapter 2: Children Behave Well If They Can

This is one of many possible ways to formulate Ross W. Greene's statement: 'Kids do well if they can'. We feel that it is the formulation with the most power. Here is a list of abilities where we as parents often have too high expectations when it comes to our children:

- the ability to calculate cause and effect in complex situations
- the ability to structure and carry out activities
- the ability to remember while thinking
- the ability to restrain impulses
- the ability to endure
- the ability to be flexible
- social skills
- sensitivity to stress
- the ability to say yes
- the ability to calm down and remain calm.

Discuss

- For which abilities have you had too high expectations of your children? Think of a few situations for each ability.

- In addition, think of some situations where things went wrong and where you can map out where your expectations were too high.

- How can you avoid similar situations in the future and instead adapt them so that the children will be able to live up to your expectations?

- Is it enough to focus on changing your expectations, or is it the way you think about your children that needs to change?

Chapter 3: Children Always Do What Makes Sense

As humans, we are greatly influenced by the situations of which we are a part, and we usually do what feels best in a given situation. We don't always think so much about what we do. The same applies to our children. The problem is that maybe they see the world with different eyes from us, and therefore act differently to what we expect.

Discuss

- Think of situations in your everyday life where, when you think about it, you can fully understand why your children did what they did.

- Also think of situations from your own life where something you did maybe wasn't what those around you expected, but you did it because it was what made most sense in that situation.

- Can you see that your behaviour in those situations was, in spite of everything, for the best in the long run?

Chapter 4: The One Who Takes Responsibility Can Make a Difference

When as parents we use a poor method with our children, we often try to pass off our responsibility, for example by blaming the children, thinking they are stubborn, annoying or the like, or by blaming the other parent.

Discuss

- Think of situations where as a parent you tried to pass off your responsibility. Do you use words like 'stubborn' and 'unmotivated' regarding your children?

- Do you as parents blame each other for the children's fighting?

Chapter 5: Children Learn Nothing from Failure

We often forget that children are used to failing. As a result, perhaps we reprimand them, make use of consequences or the like. But this unfortunately has no positive effect on them.

Discuss

- Think of situations where you have handled events based on the assumption that children learn from failure. What does that assumption mean for your everyday life?

- Do you make use of:
  - ▸ Punishments?
  - ▸ Consequences?
  - ▸ Rewards?
  - ▸ Ignoring?
  - ▸ Scolding?

- What could you do instead?

Chapter 6: You Need Self-control to Cooperate with Others

This principle is best discussed together with the next.

Chapter 7: We All Do What We Can to Maintain Self-control

We all try to retain our self-control in order to be able to interact with our surroundings in different ways. So do our children. Some children need more powerful strategies than others to be able to maintain their self-control. It could be to refuse, lie, go away, or use threats or abusive language.

Discuss

- Think of situations where what you see as behavioural problems in your children are actually only strategies on their part to retain self-control. What implications does this insight have for your future?

Chapter 8: Emotions Are Contagious

We are all affected by other people's feelings. Some children are more affected than others, because they don't know whose feeling it was in the beginning. This places great demands on us as parents and on how we handle our feelings.

Discuss

- Think of situations where your affect has passed over to your children. It could be anger or anxiety (stress), but also joy or enthusiasm.

- See if you can also find the opposite: situations where the children's affect passed over you, so that you lost your oversight and your ability to keep things together.

- Can you think of possible strategies that you could use to minimise the risk of this happening in the future?

Chapter 9: Conflicts Consist of Solutions and Failures Require a Plan

Conflicts usually start with one person having a problem that he solves. But maybe he solves it in a way that leads to a problem for someone else, which that person in turn must solve. Perhaps this leads to a new problem for the first person. And so the conflict has begun.

Discuss

- Think of situations where conflicts between you and the children have had the structure described in this principle.

- Also think of situations where your children's conflicts with their siblings or other children have taken this form. How could you have intervened in these situations? It's a good idea to think in concrete terms, based on the situations you have come up with.

Chapter 10: We Make Demands of Children That They Don't Make of Themselves – But in a Way That Works

Part of the job of being a parent is to make necessary demands of the children that they would not make of themselves. But we must make them in a way that makes the child want to fulfil them.

Discuss

- What methods do you use in everyday life to get your children to say yes? Feel free to look at the list on pages 95–99, but also try to come up with methods of your own that you use which we haven't considered.

- What distractions do you use? If you have more than one child, do you use different distractions for each child? Talk about one child at a time and jot down the distractions you use so that you have them available when the need arises.

Chapter 11: It Isn't Fair to Treat Everyone the Same

Justice means treating each child according to his particular needs.

Discuss

- Do you get a bad conscience when your children say you are unfair?

- Are you unfair?

- What special considerations do you use because they are necessary?

- How can you explain this to the children in a way that they can accept?

Chapter 12: You Become a Leader When Someone Follows You

Authority is something we as parents receive from our children, not something we take.

Discuss

- What do you do to get your children to give you authority? Talk about what concrete strategies you have.

- Do your children use abusive language? How do you react to this?

PART 2: CASES AND ACTION PLANS

Chapter 13: We Live in a Garage

Now that you have come this far, it might be a good idea to go back to the principle 'The one who takes responsibility can make a difference'.

Discuss

- How well does the garage metaphor fit your family? Do you live in a garage? In other words, do you have a tendency to:

  ▸ place responsibility on the children's lack of motivation?

  ▸ blame the children's failures on their unwillingness to cooperate?

  ▸ think that the children aren't doing the best they can in the given situation?

  ▸ use methods you are comfortable with even after being counselled that your children need different methods?

Chapter 15: The Principle of the Gentle Approach

The gentle approach is one more way for us to help our children to do what they need to do, at the same time as they feel seen and respected.

Discuss

- Think of situations where you know that you usually succeed just because you use a gentle approach. Do you go about it by:

  ▶ suggesting cooperation with the children (as in Erin's case)?

  ▶ making use of a subclause (as in Leo's case)?

- Are there times when you think you are using the gentle approach, but you are actually pussyfooting? If so, what is the reason?

  ▶ Are you afraid of the children's affect?

  ▶ Do you, at all costs, want to avoid the children getting stressed, because this is difficult for you?

- Think of a couple of situations in everyday life where you don't use a gentle approach. Try to come up with different ways to use the gentle approach in each situation.

Further Reading

In this section you can find references to the thoughts and methods presented in this book, chapter by chapter. We might repeat ourselves along the way, but only to make the connection between the principles more evident.

PART 1: PRINCIPLES

Introduction
Here we introduce the notion that children shouldn't learn to obey, but to be independent and autonomous. Alfie Kohn suggested this in the book:

> Kohn, A. (2006) *Unconditional Parenting: Moving from Rewards and Punishments to Love and Reason.* New York, NY: Atria Books.

Chapter 1: Who Has the Problem?

This chapter is based on thinking introduced by Andrew McDonnel in the book:

> McDonnel, A. (2010) *Managing Aggressive Behaviour in Care Settings.* London: Wiley.

The principle is also the basis of:

> Elvén, B.H. (2010) *No Fighting, No Biting, No Screaming: How to Make Behaving Positively Possible for People with Autism and Other Developmental Disabilities.* London: Jessica Kingsley Publishers.

Chapter 2: Children Behave Well If They Can

The quote 'Kids do well if they can' is from Ross W. Greene's book:

> Greene, R.W. (2014) *The Explosive Child: A New Approach for Understanding and Parenting Easily Frustrated, Chronically Inflexible Children.* New York, NY: Harper Paperbacks.

If you want to learn more on executive function, you can read:

> Gazzaniga, M.S., Ivry, R.B. and Mangun, G.R. (2013) *Cognitive Neuroscience.* New York, NY: W.W. Norton.

Greene keeps an updated reference list on his website (www.livesinthebalance.org).

The list of skills

The list of skills we often place high demands on is our own, but there is a lot to read on every skill:

- The ability to calculate cause and effect in complex situations

  You can find a lot of both research and theory on the subject of central coherence; for example:

  Happé, F. (2013) 'Weak Central Coherence.' In F.R. Volkmar (ed.) *Encyclopedia of Autism Spectrum Disorders*. New York, NY: Springer.

- The ability to structure and carry out activities

  Gazzaniga, M.S., Ivry, R.B. and Mangun, G.R. (2013) *Cognitive Neuroscience*. New York, NY: W.W. Norton.

- The ability to remember while thinking

  Baddeley, A. (2007) *Working Memory, Thought, and Action* (*Oxford Psychology* series). Oxford: Oxford University Press.

- The ability to restrain impulses

  Gazzaniga, M.S., Ivry, R.B. and Mangun, G.R. (2013) *Cognitive Neuroscience*. New York, NY: W.W. Norton.

- The ability to endure

  This is a great popular science article:

  Lehrer, J. (2009) 'Don't.' *The New Yorker*, 18 May 2009. Available at www.newyorker.com/reporting/2009/05/18/090518fa_fact_lehrer, accessed on 4 August 2016.

- The ability to be flexible

  This is an older definitive article:

  Scott, W.A. (1962) 'Cognitive complexity and cognitive flexibility.' *American Sociological Association* 25, 405–414.

- Social skills

Frith, U. (2003) *Autism: Explaining the Enigma*. London: Wiley.

- Sensitivity to stress
  If you really want to understand stress, we recommend that you read Chapter 4 in:

Elvén, B.H. (2010) *No Fighting, No Biting, No Screaming: How to Make Behaving Positively Possible for People with Autism and Other Developmental Disabilities*. London: Jessica Kingsley Publishers.

- The ability to say yes

DiStefano, C., Morgan, G.B. and Motl, R.W. (2012) 'An examination of personality characteristics related to acquiescence.' *Journal of Applied Measurement 13*, 1, 41–56.

- The ability to calm down and remain calm

Diekhof, E.K., Geier, K., Falkai, P. and Gruber, O. (2011) 'Fear is only as deep as the mind allows: a coordinate-based meta-analysis of neuroimaging studies on the regulation of negative affect.' *Neuroimage 58*, 1, 275–285.

Sjöwall, D., Roth, L., Lindqvist, S. and Thorell, L.B. (2013) 'Multiple deficits in ADHD: executive dysfunction, delay aversion, reaction time variability, and emotional deficits.' *Journal of Child Psychology and Psychiatry 54*, 6, 619–627.

Chapter 3: Children Always Do What Makes Sense

You can read about how physical environment affects behaviour in:

> Norman, D. (1988) *The Psychology of Everyday Things*. New York, NY: Basic Books.

On structure as a tool:

> Kabot, S. and Reeve, C. (2012) *Building Independence: How to Create and Use Structured Work Systems*. Lenexa, KS: Autism Asperger Publishing Co.

Chapter 4: The One Who Takes Responsibility Can Make a Difference

This quote is adapted from:

> Weiner, B. (1995) *Judgments of Responsibility: A Foundation for a Theory of Social Conduct*. New York, NY: Guilford Press.

Dave Dagnan's work:

> Dagnan, D. and Cairns, M. (2005) 'Staff judgements of responsibility for the challenging behaviour of adults with intellectual disabilities.' *Journal of Intellectual Disability Research 49*, 1, 95–101.

> Williams, S., Dagnan, D., Rodgers, J. and Freeston, M. (2015) 'Exploring carers' judgements of responsibility and control in response to the challenging behaviour of people with intellectual disabilities.' *Journal of Applied Research in Intellectual Disabilities 28*, 6, 589–593.

In this chapter we write about punishment. Maybe we need to clarify that we use the term 'punishment' as it is used by most people. We don't use it as it is used in behaviouristic theory. If you want to read more on the negative effects of punishment, you can read:

Gershoff, E.T. (2002) 'Corporal punishment by parents and associated child behaviors and experiences: a meta-analytic and theoretical review.' *Psychological Bulletin 128*, 4, 539–579.

Shutters, S.T. (2013) 'Collective action and the detrimental side of punishment.' *Evolutionary Psychology 11*, 2, 327–346.

Sigsgaard, E. (2005) *Scolding: Why It Hurts More Than It Helps.* New York, NY: Teachers College Press.

On legitimizing effects:

Gneezy, U. and Rustichini, A. (2000) 'A fine is a price.' *Journal of Legal Studies 29*, 1, 1–17.

On why we punish even if it doesn't work:

de Quervain, D.J.F., Fischbacher, U., Treyer, V., Schellhammer, M. *et al.* (2004) 'The neural basis of altruistic punishment.' *Science 305*, 1254–1258.

Boyd, R., Gintis, H., Bowles, S. and Richerson, P.J. (2003) 'The evolution of altruistic punishment.' *Proceedings of the National Academy of Science USA 100*, 6, 3531–3535.

In this chapter we even write about token economies and rewards. The text should not be perceived as a general critique of behaviourism. It is an evaluation of a specific method that unfortunately often fails. Some references are:

Deci, E.L., Koestner, R. and Ryan, R.M. (1999) 'A meta-analytic review of experiments examining the effects of extrinsic rewards on intrinsic motivation.' *Psychological Bulletin 125*, 6, 627–668, 692–700.

Lepper, M.R., Henderlong, J. and Gingras, I. (1999) 'Understanding the effects of extrinsic rewards on intrinsic motivation – uses and abuses of meta-analysis: comment on Deci, Koestner, and Ryan.' *Psychological Bulletin 125*, 6, 669–676.

Grolnick, W.S. (2003) *The Psychology of Parental Control: How Well-Meant Parenting Backfires.* Mahwah, NJ: Erlbaum.

Chapter 5: Children Learn Nothing from Failure
The chapter is based on the article:

van Duijvenvoorde, A.C.K., Zanolie, K., Rombouts, S.A.R.B., Raijmakers, M.E.J. and Crone, E.A. (2008) 'Evaluating the negative or valuing the positive? Neural mechanisms supporting feedback-based learning across development.' *Journal of Neuroscience 28*, 38, 9495–9503.

Chapter 6: You Need Self-control to Cooperate with Others
Original article by Kaplan and Wheeler:

Kaplan, S.G. and Wheeler, E.G. (1983) 'Survival skills for working with potentially violent clients.' *Social Casework 64*, 339–345.

Our model was first published in:

Elvén, B.H. (2010) *No Fighting, No Biting, No Screaming: How to Make Behaving Positively Possible for People with Autism and Other Developmental Disabilities*. London: Jessica Kingsley Publishers.

Other selected readings:

Diekhof, E.K., Geier, K., Falkai, P. and Gruber, O. (2011) 'Fear is only as deep as the mind allows: a coordinate-based meta-analysis of neuroimaging studies on the regulation of negative affect.' *Neuroimage 1*, 58, 275–285.

Sjöwall, D., Roth, L., Lindqvist, S. and Thorell, L.B. (2013) 'Multiple deficits in ADHD: executive dysfunction, delay aversion, reaction time variability, and emotional deficits.' *Journal of Child Psychology and Psychiatry 54*, 6, 619–627.

Wendy Grolnick's work on control, structure and autonomy you can find in:

Grolnick, W.S. (2003) *The Psychology of Parental Control: How Well-Meant Parenting Backfires*. Mahwah, NJ: Erlbaum.

Chapter 7: We All Do What We Can to Maintain Self-control

Talwar, V. and Lee, K. (2008) 'Social and cognitive correlates of children's lying behavior.' *Child Development 79*, 4, 866–881.

Talwar, V., Gordon, H.M. and Lee, K. (2007) 'Lying in the elementary school years: verbal deception and its relation to second-order belief understanding.' *Developmental Psychology 43*, 3, 804–810.

And a newer study:

Evans, A.D. and Lee, K. (2013) 'Emergence of lying in very young children.' *Developmental Psychology 49*, 10, 1958–1963.

Elvén, B.H. (2010) *No Fighting, No Biting, No Screaming: How to Make Behaving Positively Possible for People with Autism and Other Developmental Disabilities.* London: Jessica Kingsley Publishers.

A great popular science article on lying:

Bronson, P. (2008) 'Learning to Lie.' *New York Magazine*, 8 February 2008. Available at http://nymag.com/news/features/43893, accessed on 4 August 2016.

Chapter 8: Emotions Are Contagious

The concept of affect contagion comes from:

Tomkins, S. (1962) *Affect, Imagery, Consciousness Volume I.* London: Tavistock.

Tomkins, S. (1963) *Affect, Imagery, Consciousness Volume II: The Negative Affects.* New York, NY: Springer.

Tomkins, S. (1991) *Affect, Imagery, Consciousness Volume III: The Negative Affects – Anger and Fear.* New York, NY: Springer.

Scientific basis:

Hatfield, E., Cacioppo, J.T. and Rapson, R.L. (1993) 'Emotional contagion.' *Current Directions in Psychological Science 2*, 3, 96–99.

A great popular book on the subject is:

Nathanson, D.L. (1992) *Shame and Pride: Affect, Sex, and the Birth of the Self.* New York, NY: W.W. Norton.

The mirror neuron research:

Gallese, V., Fadiga, L., Fogassi, L. and Rizzolatti, G. (1994) 'Action recognition in the premotor cortex.' *Brain 119*, 2, 593–609.

Rizzolatti, G. and Craighero, L. (2004) 'The mirror-neuron system.' *Annual Review of Neuroscience 27*, 169–192.

The Daniel Stern quote is from a talk he gave at the conference Meeting of Minds in Herning, Denmark, in 2007.

The strategies for lowering the affect is from the low-arousal approach. You can read more on that in:

Elvén, B.H. (2010) *No Fighting, No Biting, No Screaming: How to Make Behaving Positively Possible for People with Autism and Other Developmental Disabilities.* London: Jessica Kingsley Publishers.

McDonnel, A. (2010) *Managing Aggressive Behaviour in Care Settings.* London: Wiley.

About keeping calm as a parent:

Koole, S.L. (2009) 'The psychology of emotion regulation: an integrative review.' *Cognition and Emotion 23*, 1, 40–41.

Jones, L., Hastings, R.P., Totsika, V., Keane, L. and Rhule, N. (2014) 'Child behavior problems and parental well-being in families of children with autism: the mediating role of mindfulness and acceptance.' *American Journal on Intellectual and Developmental Disabilities 119*, 2, 171–185.

Neece, C.L. (2014) 'Mindfulness-based stress reduction for parents of young children with developmental delays: implications for parental mental health and child behavior problems.' *Journal of Applied Research in Intellectual Disabilities 27*, 2, 174–186.

Chapter 9: Conflicts Consist of Solutions and Failures Require a Plan

Scientific documentation on restraint-related deaths:

Nunno, M.A., Holden, M.J. and Tollar, A. (2006) 'Learning from tragedy: a survey of child and adolescent restraint fatalities.' *Child Abuse & Neglect* *30*, 1333–1342.

Aiken, F., Duxbury, J., Dale, C. and Harbison, I. (2011) *Review of the Medical Theories and Research Relating to Restraint-Related Deaths.* Lancaster: Caring Solutions (UK), University of Central Lancashire.

Paterson, B., Bradley, P., Stark, C., Saddler, D., Leadbetter, D. and Allen, D. (2003) 'Deaths associated with restraint use in health and social care in the UK. The results of a preliminary survey.' *Journal of Psychiatric and Mental Health Nursing 10*, 3–15.

On how a decrease in restraints decreases injuries:

Holstead, J., Lamond, D., Dalton, J., Horne, A. and Crick, R. (2010) 'Restraint reduction in children's residential facilities: implementation at Damar Services.' *Residential Treatment for Children & Youth* *27*, 1–13.

Chapter 10: We Make Demands of Children That They Don't Make of Themselves – But in a Way That Works

Martha Nussbaum's thoughts on autonomy are given in the book:

Nussbaum, M.C. (2007) *Frontiers of Justice: Disability, Nationality, Species Membership (The Tanner Lectures on Human Values)*. Boston, MA: Harvard University Press.

On violence towards the one who sets limits:

Bjørkly, S. (1999) 'A ten-year prospective study of aggression in a special secure unit for dangerous patients.' *Scandinavian Journal of Psychology 40*, 1, 57–63.

On diversion:

Smith, R.E. (1973) 'The use of humor in the counterconditioning of anger responses: a case study.' *Behavior Therapy 4*, 4, 576–580.

McDonnel, A. (2010) *Managing Aggressive Behaviour in Care Settings*. London: Wiley.

Elvén, B.H. (2010) *No Fighting, No Biting, No Screaming: How to Make Behaving Positively Possible for People with Autism and Other Developmental Disabilities*. London: Jessica Kingsley Publishers.

On how to get a yes:

Elvén, B.H. (2010) *No Fighting, No Biting, No Screaming: How to Make Behaving Positively Possible for People with Autism and Other Developmental Disabilities*. London: Jessica Kingsley Publishers.

On validation:

Deci, E.L., Eghrari, H., Patrick, B.C. and Leone, D.R. (1994) 'Facilitating internalization: the self-determination theory.' *Journal of Personality 62,* 119–142.

Chapter 11: It Isn't Fair to Treat Everyone the Same

Our main point in this chapter is that different kids have different needs. It isn't hard to find related references. It is the basis of what we normally call differential psychology. If you want to understand the discipline, we recommend the book:

Ourth, L. and Metzler, S. (2002) *Differential Psychology: A Study of Individual Differences.* Dubuque, IA: Kendall Hunt Publishing.

Chapter 12: You Become a Leader When Someone Follows You

Hobbes' thoughts on power are from:

Hobbes, T. (1651/1982) *Leviathan.* New York, NY: Penguin Classics.

PART 2: CASES AND ACTION PLANS

The model builds on:

Kaplan, S.G. and Wheeler, E.G. (1983) 'Survival skills for working with potentially violent clients.' *Social Casework 64,* 339–345.

Whitaker, P. (2001) *Challenging Behaviour and Autism: Making Sense, Making Progress.* London: National Autistic Society.

The model was first published in:

Elvén, B.H. (2010) *No Fighting, No Biting, No Screaming: How to Make Behaving Positively Possible for People with Autism and Other Developmental Disabilities.* London: Jessica Kingsley Publishers.

The plans for conflict situations are based on a Swedish project:

Björne, P., Andresson, I., Björne, M., Olsson, M. and Pagmert, S. (2012) *Utmanande beteenden, utmanande verksamheter.* Malmö: Stadskontoret.

You can read more on physical interventions and Studio III in:

McDonnel, A. (2010) *Managing Aggressive Behaviour in Care Settings.* London: Wiley.